THE GOD
EXPERIMENT

YOUR PERSONAL JOURNEY TO TEST
THE EXTREME NATURE OF GOD

THE GOD
EXPERIMENT

JOSH AMSTUTZ

ISBN: 978-1-7377222-0-5

Published by Lakeland Community Church, N3181 State Road 67, Lake Geneva, WI 53147
lakeland.church
Printed in the United States of America

Author: Josh Amstutz
Book cover design: 16:FIFTEEN Church Media & Communications
Production and Prepress: Nei-Turner Media Group, Inc., Lake Geneva, Wisconsin

-THANKS-

This book would never have come together without many talented and gracious individuals.

First and foremost, thanks Barb Krause for taking us on a journey from manuscript to production. Without you, this book would have never happened. To Heather Koepke, thanks for your additional edits, insights, and contributions. To Richard Holt and Jen Yunker, thank you for all you do at Lakeland, and for taking my crazy ideas and making them a reality. Thanks to 16:FIFTEEN Church Media & Communications for their persistent effort with us in the cover design. Thanks to Life Together for their book design format, you've always been a great partner in seeing the local church produce the highest quality discipleship materials.

And thanks to Lisa and my family for letting me dream, and coming alongside me when I push things to the extreme. May there be many who push their faith to the extreme and discover a God who is bigger, better, and more amazing than we could ever think or imagine.

TABLE OF CONTENTS

MONTH 2: OUR IDENTITY- WHO HE SAYS WE ARE

WEEK 5- PRINCIPLES OF THE INNER IMAGE

WEEK 6- PRINCIPLES OF ROYALTY

WEEK 7- PRINCIPLES OF FAITH VS. FEAR

WEEK 8- PRINCIPLES OF FRUIT VS. FLESH

MONTH 3: ESTABLISHING YOUR IDENTITY

WHO IS THIS BOOK FOR?

You may be an atheist, an agnostic, a skeptic, a seeker, a Christian, a Muslim, a Buddhist, a whatever. You may have a faith background or not. You may have a perspective of God or no baseline at all. This book is for anyone, whether you are looking for a trial run with God, or looking to take your relationship with Him to a whole new level.

No matter who you are, where you are from, or what your current beliefs are, I believe you deserve a fair shake at figuring out who God is, and I believe He deserves a fair shake at proving Himself to you during your lifetime.

If I could challenge you in one way, I would ask, have you truly given God a fair chance in your life? Or have you just made blanket statements like, "I don't believe in God" or "God isn't relevant in my life" and left it at that? I think God deserves the opportunity to show Himself as real in your life. This book is a simple guide to afford Him that opportunity.

Nowhere along the way will your politics, sexuality, race, or religion be attacked. It's not that those things aren't real parts of our lives, or central to forming our identities, it's just that they are secondary to other more central concepts of God's identity and your identity. These central traits are where I want to give God an opportunity to reveal Himself and open your eyes to how He sees you.

My foundation for this experiment is the Bible and what it says about God, you and I. You don't have to believe the Bible to be willing to explore the concepts it reveals. But to be fair, I want you to fully know where we are launching from. You are free to explore, to doubt, to wonder, to have questions, to hopefully find answers, and perhaps even cause more questions. I'm fine with that. In many ways, I'm leaving this up to God to reveal Himself to you.

Almost 30 years ago a band called Lost Dogs wrote a song that captures the essence of how I want you to be able to experience God. The song lyrics are as follows, and I hope you find yourself somewhere in this song and invited into the journey of 'breathing deep.'

"Breathe Deep (The Breath of God)"

Politicians, morticians, philistines, homophobes,
Skinheads, deadheads, tax evaders, street kids,
Alcoholics, workaholics, wise guys, dim-wits,
Blue-collars, white-collars, war-mongers, peace-nicks.

Breathe deep,
Breathe deep the Breath of God,
Breathe deep,
Breathe deep the Breath of God.

Suicidals, rock idols, shut-ins, drop-outs,
Friendless, homeless, penniless and depressed,
Presidents, residents, foreigners and aliens,
Dissidents, feminists, xenophobes and chauvinists.

Breathe deep,
Breathe deep the Breath of God,
Breathe deep,
Breathe deep the Breath of God.

Evolutionists, creationists, perverts, slum lords,
Dead-beats, athletes, Protestants and Catholics,
Housewives, neophytes, pro-choice, pro-life,
Misogynists, monogamists, philanthropists, blacks and whites.

Breathe deep,
Breathe deep the Breath of God,
Breathe deep,
Breathe deep the Breath of God.

Police, obese, lawyers, and government,
Sex offenders, tax collectors, war vets, rejects,
Atheists, scientists, racists, sadists,
Biographers, photographers, artists, pornographers.

Breathe deep,
Breathe deep the Breath of God,
Breathe deep,
Breathe deep the Breath of God.

Gays and lesbians, demagogues and thespians,
The disabled, preachers, doctors and teachers,
Meat eaters, wife beaters, judges and juries,
Long-hair, no-hair, everybody everywhere.

Breathe deep,
Breathe deep the Breath of God,
Breathe deep,
Breathe deep the Breath of God

Breathe deep,
Breathe deep the Breath of God,
Breathe deep,
Breathe deep the Breath of God

Reprinted with permission from Lo-Fidelity Records

INTRODUCTION

Every summer, my family took a vacation to the northwoods of Wisconsin. We spent just about every minute we could in the water—playing, swimming, relaxing, but most importantly for my family: skiing. Water skiing was basically a rite of passage for us. Some of the most important moments were when you got up skiing for the first time, when you slalomed for the first time (skiing on one ski), the first time you skied beside someone, the first time you crossed the wake, and for many, the "firsts" continued on with skiing backward, skiing on anything that could float, barefooting, trick skiing, going off the ski jump, wakeboarding, wake surfing, knee boarding... basically if we could ride it behind a boat, we did.

But at the heart of it was always our desire to push the limits a little further. To see how far we could push ourselves, our equipment and our spirits. And it was always rewarded with great applause, the honking of the boat horn, and usually a back rub at the end of the day to soothe all those hurting muscles from a day of pushing ourselves to the extreme.

I've carried that mindset throughout my entire life. For some, like myself, the drive to push things to the limit may be a little more hard-wired into us. That drive, that "leap of faith" mentality, has physically impacted me as I've had my share of broken bones, pulled muscles, torn tendons, and more concussions than I should. However, it's also that drive, the testing of limits, the pushing of myself to the extremes, that has led me to all of the great accomplishments I've been able to experience.

The mindset to push things to the limit is not only present in what I can do physically. That natural drive has also always been a part of my spiritual journey. As a result, in the same way I might push myself physically to the limit, I've also taken "leaps of faith" spiritually many times over and have seen God show up in profound and personal ways.

The biggest thing I've learned in my nearly 40 years of having a personal relationship with God is that the more I get to know Him, the more I realize there is still so much to be discovered.

I love how C.S. Lewis portrayed this in his *Chronicles of Narnia* series in an encounter between Lucy and Aslan (who is the lion and the representation of God throughout the series). Lucy's perspective is that Aslan has grown significantly. He goes on to correct her, as it has not he who has grown, but Lucy has. And each year she grows, he will also grow.

That has been so true throughout my life. The more I have grown in my walk with the Lord, the bigger He is. It seems like every time I have an "Aha!" moment with the Lord, in the very same moment there is this overwhelming feeling within my spirit that what I just discovered or experienced about God is only the tip of the iceberg.

We see throughout scripture that the vastness of God is bigger than we could ever imagine. Consider these verses...

8 "'For my thoughts are not your thoughts,
   neither are your ways my ways,'
      declares the Lord.
9 'As the heavens are higher than the earth,
   so are my ways higher than your ways
   and my thoughts than your thoughts."
ISAIAH 55:8-9

"Do you not know?
   Have you not heard?
The Lord is the everlasting God,
   the Creator of the ends of the earth.
He will not grow tired or weary,
   and his understanding no one can fathom."
ISAIAH 40:28

33 "Oh, the depth of the riches of the wisdom and knowledge of God!
   How unsearchable his judgments,
   and his paths beyond tracing out!
34 'Who has known the mind of the LORD?
   Or who has been His counselor?'"

ROMANS 11:33-34

"'Can you fathom the mysteries of God?
   Can you probe the limits of the Almighty?"

JOB 11:7

Up until now you might think, "It seems like God is unfathomable; no one can discover the fullness of Him." And while it is true that we will never discover all the fullness of who He is in our lifetime, there is another fascinating verse in the book of Proverbs that prods us to go after it. All of it... all of Him.

"It is the glory of God to conceal a matter;
   to search out a matter is the glory of kings."

PROVERBS 25:2

Now initially, the concept of God hiding things from us may sound cruel, but not after you read the next part of the verse: "It is the glory of kings to search out a matter." Simply put, it is mankind's greatest accomplishment and glory to search out and discover the things placed here **for us** by God.

Picture it like an Easter egg hunt. When parents hide Easter eggs for their children, they don't hide them in such a way that the children will never find them, they hide them with the intent and joy of watching their children search and eventually find what was hidden FOR them. Both the parents who are hiding the eggs and the kids who are searching desire the same thing. But the fun and the joy is in the search and the personal discovery.

I believe God has humanity on a God-sized Easter egg hunt. But instead of looking for eggs, we are looking for Him. And once we find Him the search is not over... instead it is just the beginning. It's the beginning of discovering His character, His view of us and His plans for us.

And that's a lot, because you'll never discover it all. God says there is always more. So here is where taking things to the extreme can be incredibly fruitful. If there is more of God, His view of us, and His plans for us than we will ever discover in our lifetime, then we must be efficient with the time we have here on earth to do what we can to discover as much of it as possible.

This is where the God Experiment begins. In the same way that I used to push myself physically to the limits to see how far I could take things skiing, I want to challenge each and every one of us to **push our faith to the extreme limits to test the extreme nature of God.**

In many ways, to use a poker term, I'm going "all in" on God showing up and showing off in your life. I'm betting everything on Him being who He says He is, and doing what He says He will do.

The beauty of this experiment is it is for EVERYONE.

It is for me (a follower of Jesus for 40 years) to discover more about God and who He is and who He says I am.

It is for the Christ follower who is growing, for the Christ follower who is doubting, for the Christ follower just starting their journey or the one who has been on it for a long time.

It is for the person who walked away from their faith long ago, but has wondered if there was more that they never experienced.

It is for the person who has done the "unspeakable." That's right, you. You who have said to yourself, "I might be interested in God, but I know He wants nothing to do with me."

It is for the atheist. Yep, that's right, the person who doesn't believe in God at all.

It is for the seeker, the doubter, the skeptic, and the believer. Because in any experiment you start by making a hypothesis. The hypothesis is the individual's best guess of what they think the experiment will produce. But, no matter the hypothesis, the experiment will produce an outcome. And we're going to test God and see what He produces as an outcome.

As we begin this God Experiment, each of us has a hypothesis of how we believe God will show up or not show up. How God will prove to be true or not prove to be true. However, if you are willing to embrace the fullness of this experiment, I'm going to trust God will do His part.

So what am I asking of you during the God Experiment?

Simply this: join me on a discovery journey looking for the extreme nature of God. Each day we're going to be looking at different aspects of God. Some days will be about who God is, other days will be about who He says we are, and others will be about how we live our lives.

On each day we're going to dive into one simple aspect of God. During that day, I'm asking you to push yourself and push God to the limit. Take the concept as far as you can take it.

For some, we might call this exercising our faith.

If you are an individual who wouldn't claim to have faith, then consider it like an Easter egg hunt where you are looking for God (perhaps even very skeptically), but do your best to give God a fair shake at showing up in your life as you look for Him around the subject of the day.

Let me give you an example before we begin. I've heard hundreds of songs about the love of God throughout my life. Some of them could be passed off as a sappy love song between any two people. They are about love that is deeper than the ocean, higher than the mountains, farther reaching than the east is from the west, burning so deeply that flowing rivers could not quench it… you get the point. It's grand, it's vast, it's big.

If that's true, there is always more to be discovered about the love of God. So, if our subject for the day is God's love, let's look at one aspect of the love of God from Isaiah 54:10.

It says, "'Though the mountains be shaken and the hills be removed, yet my unfailing love for you will not be shaken nor my covenant of peace be removed,' says the LORD, who has compassion on you."

In that verse we see an attribute about His love. That attribute is that it is unfailing and unshaken. It will never be removed.

Have you ever experienced conditional love? You probably have, at some point in your life, from a friend, a sibling, or a parent. That love might crumble and be shaken or removed, but God will never stop loving you.

What would it look like to take that idea to the extreme? What would it look like in a 24-hour time period to exercise your faith to the extreme, or, like an Easter egg hunt, to look for it, to seek it, to see, and experience how God's love is unshakable?

If you're a Christian, take your faith to the next level and remind yourself of this statement throughout the day: "God's love is not failing in my life. His love is not shaken from me by anything I do or say."

If you're the seeker, the non-believer, or the skeptic, let's call your Easter egg hunt your "Skeptic's Challenge/Prayer" because that is what you're testing God for. You're embracing the challenge, testing to see if He is real, if He is there, if this concept could be true of Him, and if there is something for you to discover about God that could make any difference in your life.

So in regard to the concept in Isaiah 54:10, that His love for you is unshakable, you might embrace your challenge this way:

Look all day long for anything that would be unique or unusual in your life that could be God trying to get your attention. Look for someone or something God might be using to tell you He has always been there for you, His love for you has never left, and there is nothing you can do to make His love stop chasing after you.

For your sake and for God's sake, give this your all. Every hour, simply remind yourself what you're looking for, who God is, or who He says you are. Believe it with all your heart, look for it with all your heart. Take it to the extreme… because it's at the extremes where we break barriers. When we push ourselves to the extreme physically in athletics we break barriers and when we push ourselves spiritually to the extreme we break spiritual barriers in our journey with God.

What could your life look like a few months from now if you simply took a few minutes every day to set your mind and your heart on a treasure hunt? The thing you are hunting for is God. And if God is as extraordinary as He says He is, He may just do something incredibly extraordinary in you.

Welcome to the God Experiment!

NOTES

CHARACTER TRAITS OF GOD

WEEK ONE

WEEK ONE / DAY ONE

GOD IS HOLY

"...Day and night they never stop saying:
'Holy, holy, holy
is the LORD God Almighty,
who was, and is, and is to come.'"

REVELATION 4:8b

If you grew up going to church, maybe you've heard that word a time or two. But if you're like me, you sang the word "Holy" hundreds of times but had no idea what it really meant. And you still may not have a grasp of its true meaning.

Holy means sacred, set apart, revered, or divine. I am often drawn to that second definition—set apart—because God is. He is set apart in every aspect of life. As soon as I think I have an understanding of God, I start to see how much bigger and set apart He is from my version that I've imagined or created of Him in my mind.

As we dive into this God Experiment, I believe we will discover that God is set apart in every way imaginable. My hope is that we will catch a glimpse of the depth of God in how set apart He is.

In Revelation 4:8b we get to peer into the throneroom of God. There we see four amazing angels who "Day and night... never stop saying: 'Holy, holy, holy is the LORD God Almighty,' who was, and is, and is to come."

If these are the words that are being spoken endlessly day and night in the throneroom of God, then they must accurately describe God. The word *holiness* refers to His separateness, His otherness, the fact that He is unlike any other being. It indicates His complete and infinite perfection.

For us, we spend our lives trying to make things fit into boxes so they make sense to us. We create strategic plans for almost everything in life to manage our situations, our relationships, our finances, our jobs, our marriages, our families, our hobbies, our everything. But what if God is bigger and outside and set apart from all of those things? What if He Himself doesn't fit into any one box?

My wife and I have nine kids. Yes, they are all ours (my wife gave birth to all nine)... no, we don't homeschool... no, we're not Catholic... yes, we know how it happens... and yes, we drive a very stylish 12-passenger van.

As they grow I know this means I'm on a trajectory to eventually have nine additional drivers in my house. Currently, we have four kids driving, with another one on her way to having a license within the next year.

One of the things that is amusing to me is my kids' sense of direction as they learn to drive. My kids are growing up in the era of GPS and cell phones. They have never had to really know where anything is, they simply plug their desired destination into their GPS and follow the arrow that represents their car.

I grew up in the era of maps. Remember those? Those things made of paper that folded like a complex origami puzzle, that you stored in your glove compartment. You even had multiple maps, one for this city and one for that, one for this state and one for that.

We used maps to create our own route to our destination; we did not follow a computer's directions. We studied maps, memorized the primary roads and then we just went for it. I used to drive places all the time saying to myself, "if I head this direction, I'll eventually hit such-and-such road." The point is, we always knew there were many ways to get to the same destination. Lots of different roads we could take. Unfortunately, today my kids usually only know one way to their destinations. It's like they've only experienced a small, minute portion of the whole map.

What if the same is actually true of God in your life? What if we have a tendency to only see God one way? Or, only see a small portion of who He is? What if you, like most of us, have a tendency to box God in? What if the truth is that as soon as you think you've figured God out and boxed Him in, He will knock down those walls and show you there is no box. Is it possible you primarily see only one way, one view to who God is? What if you could see more of the whole map?

DAILY DISCOVERY: Today the experiment is simple. Let's assume God is bigger and outside of your plan, your understanding of Him, and your perspective. Our view of His purity is too small. Our view of His love is too small. Our view of His wisdom, His goodness, and His grace is too small. All of it is just a small portion of this HOLY and set apart God. Maybe a simple prayer leading you on your daily discovery could be, "God, show me today in some way how Holy and set apart you are."

SKEPTIC'S CHALLENGE/ PRAYER: Perhaps the very first place you could start on this journey would be to simply ask God to show Himself as real to you. Would you consider looking today for evidence of God's presence in your life? Is it possible He's been there, but just outside of the box you might expect Him to be in?

NOTES

WEEK ONE / DAY TWO

GOD IS GOOD

"Taste and see that the LORD is good..."

PSALM 34:8

O ne of my favorite movies growing up was "Monty Python and the Search for the Holy Grail." In one scene, God is portrayed as an old man with a beard, sitting on a throne, peering through the clouds and yelling at humanity with a bitter British accent. It's a really funny scene from a cinematic perspective, but I don't think it's even remotely close to who God is.

Yet, many people probably carry that same view of God. Like He is an angry old man on a throne just waiting to smite someone for sinning.

The truth is, there is sin, and sin has left things broken. Thus, we live in a broken world, where relationships fail and our bodies fail, and there is real hurt and pain we will all experience. But the reality of brokenness in our world does not change the character of God.

There are dozens of verses reminding us of His goodness even in the midst of our struggles and pain.

"Surely your goodness and love will follow me
 all the days of my life..."

PSALM 23:6

"I remain confident of this:
 I will see the goodness of the LORD
 in the land of the living."

PSALM 27:13

"Answer me, LORD, out of the goodness of your love..."
PSALM 69:16

I could go on and on.

But even the first verse for today is really an invitation: "Taste and see that the LORD is good." It is not just a statement about who He is or what He has. It's more than that. It's what He has for you, and what He wants you to experience. It's an invitation to taste His goodness, to see it and experience it personally.

In my life, I've experienced the goodness of God time and time again, sometimes in small and subtle ways and sometimes in miraculous, life-saving ways.

One of the first times I can clearly recall God demonstrating His goodness to Lisa and me was by simply meeting our needs. It was early in our marriage; we were poor and just getting by. Then one morning our washing machine died. I remember looking at our bank account, knowing we didn't have the money to buy a new one or even a used one. I think I prayed the most simplistic prayer that morning; maybe you've prayed it before: "God, HELP!" That was it. It wasn't long or impressive, but it was honest.

That night we had dinner plans with some of our closest friends. While catching up one of us must have shared that our washer had died that morning. To our amazement, our friends said to us, "Well, do you need a new one?" Well duh... of course we did!

My friend, who was also a youth pastor, went on to tell me that the night before, his youth group students had gone on a "bigger or better" hunt. That's where each team starts with a penny and goes door-to-door asking strangers if they would trade for something bigger or better than what they currently have. So the penny gets traded for an apple, the apple gets traded for a book, the book gets traded for a blown-out basketball, the basketball gets traded for a broken TV, the TV gets traded, and so on. Well, one team traded all the way up to a brand new, never used, still with original tags, washing machine. My buddy led us out into his garage and said, "We ended up with this washer and we had no idea what to do with it. It's yours!"

And just like that, what seemed like a huge hurdle to overcome was resolved in less than 12 hours. All I could say that night was, "God is so good." He knew my need before I did, and helped meet my need a day before I even knew I needed it.

Taste and see that the Lord is GOOD.

You may question if God is good. Maybe you've experienced some serious pain or hurt in your life. This is the reality for all of humanity in a broken and sinful world. Yet God and His goodness is still in the midst of it all and He desires for you to personally experience His goodness in the midst of your trials.

I can find joy in every day, not because life is always good, but because God is.

DAILY DISCOVERY: Today's experiment is to ask God to show His goodness to you today. It may be small and subtle or blatant and unmistakable. But I believe God is good. And the experiment of the day is simple: taste and see that God is good.

SKEPTIC'S CHALLENGE/ PRAYER: Perhaps you've seen things in your life that seem to just work out for your good. Is it possible God might be behind some of those moments? Perhaps you could ask for God to do something subtle (or blatant) that would be evidence of His goodness to you today.

NOTES

WEEK ONE / DAY THREE

GOD IS GRACIOUS

"The LORD is gracious and compassionate,
  slow to anger and rich in love."

PSALM 145:8

Growing up, one of my favorite things to do was to visit my grandparents. For one set of grandparents who lived in a retirement community, it was because I loved playing in their community rec room with pool tables, shuffleboard, ping pong, and a massive assortment of board games. For my other grandparents, one of the things I loved most was my grandmother's chocolate eclairs.

They were my favorite. And every time, without fail, she would make them for me. I don't know if everyone else loved them to the extent that I did. After I grew up and got married, if Lisa and I were swinging by even for a half hour, she would still have a pan of chocolate eclairs waiting for me as we walked in the door.

I never did anything to deserve them, and I never asked for them, but they were always there for me like clockwork.

God's grace is the same way: we never deserved it, we didn't even initially ask for it, and yet it's been there like clockwork for us, time and time again.

Grace is getting what we don't deserve. The Greek word that gets translated as 'grace' can also be translated as 'gift.' In some passages of the Bible that is exactly how it is translated. It's a gift. And it seems like God is a gift-giving God.

God **gave** His one and only Son: Jesus **gave** His life for us. And God offers us a free **gift** of forgiveness through faith in Jesus. He **gives** His

Holy Spirit to guide us in life. He **gives** spiritual gifts. And He offers us grace daily. Good things, sweet things, that we don't deserve — time after time.

The amazing thing is, grace is a gift that costs eveything for the giver and nothing for the recipient. And that is exactly what God has done. He has paid what is necessary to grace us with what we need.

Sometimes the good gifts He offers are patience, peace, joy, hope, or strength. Sometimes it's a practical need. Sometimes it is a very impractical gift, but it's obvious it's from Him.

If you're a parent, you probably understand the idea of grace. Most parents want to give their children the world, even if their children did nothing in the first place to deserve it. They want to give them life experiences, they want to give them clothing, good food, good hobbies, etc. Parents will sacrifice time and treasure to get their kids the sports equipment they need, the instrument and lessons they want, or the education they hope for. They will do anything to help their kids get ahead and do well in life.

I imagine we as parents picked that up from our Heavenly Father who, in the same way, is always wanting to grace us or gift us with something we do not deserve.

DAILY DISCOVERY: Is it possible that God has more grace for you than you could even imagine? Is it possible for you to experience the richness of His grace in your life today? Call it an experiment or call it faith, let's head into today assuming God has a special grace (gift) for you today. Look for it and make sure to journal where you saw His grace.

SKEPTIC'S CHALLENGE/ PRAYER: Is it possible that God wants to give you something good today? Is there an area in your life where you need grace to handle the situation? Write down where you need grace, and then let's ask God to do something in your life that would be a reflection of the grace you need in that situation. It could be a simple prayer like this: *'God, I need some grace to handle this situation. Would you give me favor in this situation or grace that is an obvious good gift from you?'*

NOTES

WEEK ONE / DAY FOUR

GOD IS MERCIFUL

"The LORD is gracious and merciful,

slow to anger and abounding in steadfast love."

PSALM 145:8 (ESV)

Just as in this verse, grace and mercy often go together. Sometimes the two words can almost be used interchangeably and yet they are quite different. Here's how I often say it to remind folks how they are different:

Grace is getting what you don't deserve.

Mercy is not getting what you do deserve.

Picture it like this. My family lives close to multiple beaches on Geneva Lake in southern Wisconsin. Sometimes with the nature of young kids, you try to have these fun family experiences and life seems to throw curve balls your way. Just picture it. We've packed beach towels, toys, beach chairs, food, drinks, etc.; way too much stuff for a few hours at the beach. But not too long after arriving, some young child starts to have a bad attitude about something in life and nothing seems to turn their attitude around. They are crying, or screaming, or whining, or teasing and making the whole experience less than favorable for not only our family but other beachgoers as well. Now, what that child deserves is a good punishment for their behavior and attitude.

As I pull them aside and start to talk through their punishment, they become reasonable. Not only that, they apologize. Not the fake, I'm sorry-but-really-didn't-mean-it apology. We've all seen that before. But a true apology. Now it doesn't make their previous behavior okay, but now as a parent you're at a crossroads. There are times when, to help the child learn their lesson, we will still enforce a punishment. But on this occasion I offer mercy. They are not going to receive what they deserve, which is a punishment. Then, while driving home from the beach, I decide to stop by the local ice cream shop and get everyone ice cream. That's grace, getting something they didn't deserve.

Grace is when you get the good things you don't deserve. Mercy is when you're spared from the bad things you do deserve. God is generous with both. But for today, let's consider mercy. One of my favorite set of verses on mercy is:

22 "The steadfast love of the LORD never ceases;
    his mercies never come to an end;
23 they are new every morning;
    great is your faithfulness."
LAMENTATIONS 3:22-23 (ESV)

I don't know if you've ever blown it in life and needed a "do over." You needed mercy. The amazing thing about His mercy is that there is a new amount of it for you on a daily basis. Did you see it? His mercies are new every morning. That means even if every day you wake up and you feel like you blew it in life, He offers us mercy. He lets us "off the hook" spiritually speaking.

I can't tell you how many times I've thought to myself, "Thank you God, that your mercies are new every day." God's mercies show up in lots of different ways. It's not being pulled over when you're speeding down the highway, it's passing the test that you didn't study for, it's pulling together the deal at work when you really didn't do the work. You've probably heard the phrase, "That worked out in spite of me." It's the recognition that something bad didn't happen in spite of what you did.

This past summer, I was pulling my boat out of a lake on our trailer and before driving it out, I forgot to pull up the motor. When I drove it out, the motor was literally missing the ground by an inch. It was a complete miracle that I didn't wreck the prop or the motor by leaving it down. It's just mercy. I didn't receive what I deserved, which was probably an expensive bill for my mistake.

DAILY DISCOVERY: If you're honest with yourself, no matter how good you are, there are places you've blown it in life. Mistakes you've made with others and with yourself, and yet God's mercies are new every morning. Today, look for His mercy in your life. Let's assume He has an enormous amount of mercy for you today: will you discover it?

SKEPTIC'S CHALLENGE/ PRAYER: Can you name a time or two you didn't get what you deserved? You can probably name way more than two. Maybe it was a mistake you've made with others or with yourself and yet you were "lucky" and didn't get what you deserved. Today, look for His mercy in your life. Let's assume He has an enormous amount... will you discover it?

NOTES

WEEK ONE / DAY FIVE

GOD IS FORGIVING

"You, LORD, are forgiving and good,

abounding in love to all who call to you."

PSALM 86:5

"If we confess our sins, he is faithful and just and will forgive us our sins and purify us from all unrighteousness."

1 JOHN 1:9

As a parent, I regularly walk through the hurts that happen between my children. "He's teasing," "He stole my toy," "She hit me," and around and around it goes. As such, we say a lot of "I'm sorry's" at our house. But you probably know someone who says they are sorry, but their heart is not in it.

I always say the same thing: "This time say it like you mean it." Because that's what matters in helping the offended child to forgive. And forgiveness is huge. It's letting someone else off the hook for their wrong and no longer holding the offense against them.

Now when it comes to God, depending on your journey with Him, you may or may not even see the need for forgiveness. Maybe you don't think that there is anything broken at a cosmic or spiritual level that would demand forgiveness to be offered or received.

If you don't believe in God, or would call yourself a skeptic or seeker, that's perfectly fine. Let me simply share what the Bible says and then you can decide for yourself if there is anything you want to do about it or explore within it.

Romans 3:23 says, "... for all have sinned..." That's pretty self-explanatory.

It is basically calling out the spiritual state of humanity. We all have done wrong to one another and God.

Wrongdoing deserves punishment. From a Biblical perspective the punishment for sin is steep.

"For the wages of sin is death, but the gift of God is eternal life in Christ Jesus our LORD." ROMANS 6:23

Now, you might think death is way too steep of a price to pay for sin. I agree it's a crazy high standard of punishment, but God took it all into account and paid that price for you.

"For God so loved the world that he gave his one and only Son, that whoever believes in him shall not perish but have eternal life." JOHN 3:16

Simply put, God loved you so much that He sent His Son. And Jesus willingly laid down His life for you and me at the cross to pay that really steep price for sin. All you and I do is receive the forgiveness that is offered to us.

That's why when I think about this character trait, 'God is forgiving,' it's like the understatement of the century, and of all time, for that matter.

There is another amazing verse in scripture:

"But God demonstrates his own love for us in this: While we were still sinners, Christ died for us." ROMANS 5:8

I don't know if you caught it. If Christ died for us while we were still sinners, it means Christ was making a way for forgiveness long before we were ever sorry. Long before you or I ever thought about God, had ever done wrong, or had ever felt bad for doing wrong, He was already offering forgiveness.

Not long ago, one of my daughters (away at college) got in a small fender bender with another car parked in her driveway. She called me, a little freaked out as most teenagers would be. I called my insurance agent, got the ball rolling for the claim, and went to sleep that night. I texted her to let her know everything was being taken care of and she might hear from the insurance company if they had additional questions.

The next day, she called sounding hysterical and still fighting back tears on the phone. Over and over she apologized and kept saying, "I feel horrible." And I kept assuring her it would be okay, this is why we have insurance.

For half an hour I tried to talk her off the mental cliff she was on, beating herself up for the accident. Now, while it was true that yes it was her fault, and yes it is my car, and yes my insurance premium will go up, at the end of the day beating yourself up for what the insurance is covering is ignoring what the insurance is there for.

I've talked with plenty of people who carry shame, guilt, or sorrow for sin that they are trying to figure out how to deal with on their own. When they do so, they are missing the point of Christ's death on the cross. He paid a price to offer forgiveness so we don't have to live in those feelings any longer.

When we receive His forgiveness, it is like walking out of the prison cell that He unlocked for us 2,000 years ago at the cross.

Like my daughter who was living with a tension that she didn't need to carry any more, God offers forgiveness so we don't have to live in the tension of our sin anymore.

DAILY DISCOVERY: Is there anything in your life where you're still beating yourself up but God has let you off the hook?

SKEPTIC'S CHALLENGE/ PRAYER: If you wouldn't call yourself a Christian, today simply ask yourself this question. "If God is real and made a way for forgiveness, is there anything I would ever want forgiveness for?" Is there anything you think is not forgivable? Why? Do you have any basis for that other than it's just what you've always thought?

NOTES

WEEK ONE / DAY SIX & SEVEN

SEEK AND SIMMER

"May these words of my mouth and this meditation of my heart
   be pleasing in your sight..."

PSALM 19:14

"so is my word that goes out from my mouth:
   It will not return to me empty,
but will accomplish what I desire
   and achieve the purpose for which I sent it."

ISAIAH 55:11

There is something profound in letting a verse or truth from God simmer in your soul. This is real Biblical meditation. Sometimes when we think of meditation we think of the practice of meditation in Eastern religions, which is often the emptying of your mind. Biblical meditation is the complete opposite. It is the filling of your mind and the purposeful "rethinking" of a good or true thought.

Over the next two days, write down an idea, verse, or concept that you want to think (or rethink) about. What do you want to let your soul simmer in for a bit longer?

DAY 6: LET THAT THOUGHT SIMMER

What idea was most challenging this week?

DAY 7: LET THAT THOUGHT SIMMER

What day or concept do you want to rethink about?

....

....

....

....

....

NOTES

....

....

....

....

....

....

....

....

....

WEEK TWO

WEEK TWO / DAY ONE

GOD IS FAITHFUL

"Know therefore that the LORD your God is God; he is the faithful God, keeping his covenant of love to a thousand generations of those who love him and keep his commandments."

DEUTERONOMY 7:9

I am blessed to have parents who have been married for 50 years. This is definitely not the norm in our culture. Every once in a while as a kid, while flipping through the channels on TV, I would run across shows like Phil Donahue that seemed to thrive on conflict-based reality television. The title of the show would be "Caught Cheating." And live on air people would confront their spouses and lovers with the new knowledge of these affairs and unfaithful relationships. And of course all hell would break loose on the show, and likely the crazier the responses from the people, the higher the ratings for the show.

When I would catch a minute of the show, as a kid I was honestly confused and dumbfounded. Probably because of my parents' faithful relationship, it was always so strange to me, the idea of people mistreating their marriages and relationships so flippantly. To this day I still can't watch a TV show or a movie that has an affair in it. My wife knows this and has always graciously changed channels or left movies in the theater. I just can't stand the unfaithfulness.

You may have grown up in the complete opposite setting where faithful relationships were illusive and unheard of. And while I value faithful relationships through and through, if I'm honest, I can't tell you the number of times I've been unfaithful in my relationship with God. Like most, I become distracted with the "shiny" things of the world. My love for those things starts to crowd out my love for God.

Yet God is faithful, yesterday, today, and forever.

Throughout the Bible, God makes covenants with man. Covenants are promises; some that He makes are conditional and some are unconditional. The conditional promises usually have to do with blessings. For example, God said in the Old Testament that if we keep His commands and do not turn to other gods, then His favor will remain on us. However, there are many promises that have nothing to do with our actions, they are just God's promises that He will forever keep regardless of our behavior. These are His unconditional covenants. They are many and they are true. There are more than 3,000 promises from God to humanity throughout scripture. The amazing thing is He has never broken one of His more than 3,000 promises. He is faithful and true to His Word and His promises.

Here's the crazy part: whether you believe in God or not, He has made promises to you. Promises that you can trust.

I know there are some who don't ever want to take a leap of faith with God because they don't see God as a trustworthy God. Last week, we spent a day pondering the goodness of God. The truth is, if God is good and He is faithful, then trusting His promises and trusting Him is a good bet.

You're not trying out your trust on a tyrannical ruler, or a domineering Lord, but a good, gracious, merciful, forgiving, faithful God.

I like that phrase: try out your trust. Maybe you and I could push our trust muscles to new limits today.

Author A.W. Pink said, "No one ever yet really trusted Him in vain."

I don't believe you will be wasting your time, or your effort will be in vain as you "try out your trust" and wait upon God to test His faithfulness. If He is truly faithful, then of all experiments to push to the limits, it is this one. Either He is a promise keeper or He is not.

The 19th century preacher Charles Spurgeon said, "There is no saint here who can out-believe God. God never out-promised Himself yet."

DAILY DISCOVERY: What could you do today to try out your trust? What promise from God are you most interested in seeing Him fulfill?

SKEPTIC'S CHALLENGE/ PRAYER: Has there ever been a time when you thought God was with you or helping you (He was faithful to you) even when you did nothing to deserve it? If you are a spiritual skeptic, maybe a simple prayer for you today is, *"God, I'm keeping my eye out for you today; looking for evidence of you as a faithful promise keeper."* What could it mean for you today to try out your trust?

NOTES

WEEK TWO / DAY TWO

GOD IS WISE

"Oh, the depth of the riches both of the wisdom and knowledge of God!

How unsearchable his judgments,

and his paths beyond tracing out!"

ROMANS 11:33

Have you ever done anything in the past that, looking back now, you know was really foolish?

Nearly 20 years ago, as a youth pastor, I took a group of middle school students on a weekend caving trip in Indiana. We stayed overnight at a local church that was gracious enough to let a massive group of preteens crash on their floor for an evening. Of course before turning in, we played group games late into the night. During those games there are always "good guys" and "bad guys" and some form of jail that you get thrown into if you get caught, and some flag or goal you're trying to get to. That night, I found myself being chased by a middle school girl as we neared the end of the game. I was already exhausted from hours of play. As this young girl chased me, I realized she was going to catch me — and I couldn't let that happen. I couldn't be caught by a little girl. So I did what any youth pastor would do who is running on 2 a.m. adrenaline and a diet cola. I happened to be in the upper balcony of the church and I was running right next to the railing. To escape being caught, I jumped right over that railing mid-sprint.

Now as I soared through the air (it's amazing what you can think of during that half-second), I'm pretty sure I was thinking, "I must look like the most amazing youth pastor right now flying through the air!" That thought came to a crashing halt as *I* came to a crashing halt on the concrete floor below. And that crash was very literal. When I landed, I came down entirely on my left heel and shattered it on impact.

The pain was excruciating; my foot blew up to the size of a football, months of surgery and rehab would lie ahead of me and I still have pain associated with that injury today. I don't remember much from the next day due to the meds the doctors put me on, but what I remember clearly was calling my wife the next morning and starting my conversation with "Don't be mad at me, but I did something kind of foolish."

Foolish actions can have lifelong repercussions. Jumping off that balcony was one of mine. It's amazing what one foolish decision can do in your life. That one helped me see I was not invincible. Since then, I like to think I really do process my decisions in order to make the wise call.

One of the attributes of God that I've come to appreciate more is God's wisdom. I realized long ago that God has a best plan or wise decision for everything I face in life.

While there will be some things we will never understand or be able to fathom about God's ways, there are many other things that because God is good and simply kind to us, He willingly shares with His children.

Not long ago, our dishwasher stopped working. Or at least after it finished it was always filled with standing water at the bottom. I knew something was wrong but I didn't know what. And I'm not a small appliance repairman, but I'm generally handy, so I started taking it apart to see if I could fix it. However, before I started I took a moment to throw up one of those quick prayers. It was a little bit more elaborate than "God, help!" It was, "God give me your wisdom to solve this problem. You know what is wrong. Show me."

As I stared at the internal mechanics of the dishwasher, I felt like God made every part disappear except for one part that I found myself just staring at. So I decided to try to take that one part off. Sure enough, as I pulled off the part, out came a small piece of a toy that had fallen into the dishwasher and clogged the mechanism from draining the water.

And just like that, it was fixed. As I put the dishwasher back in place, my wife was amazed as I looked like the handiest husband on the planet. But the truth was simply this: God knew exactly what the problem was and exactly how to fix it. He had wisdom for the situation, and I just needed the wisdom He had.

I've said this a handful of times about the wisdom of God: There is no earthly problem that God does not have a heavenly solution for.

Think about that. There is no problem that you are facing that God doesn't have a best solution for. God has a solution for the traffic problem of your city, He has a solution for the staffing issue at your place of work, He has a solution for the healing of that broken relationship, He has a solution for the financial pickle you've gotten yourself into, He has a solution for every question you have and every problem you face.

In fact, wisdom is one trait that the Bible encourages us to boldly and audaciously ask for.

"If any of you lacks wisdom, you should ask God, who gives generously to all without finding fault, and it will be given to you." JAMES 1:5

I don't know where you need wisdom today, but today's experiment may be one of the most fun yet.

DAILY DISCOVERY: There is no earthly problem that God does not have a heavenly solution for. Where could you use wisdom today? Let's assume God has a great solution for the problem you need to solve. Maybe your simple prayer is, *"God, please give me a complete or even partial solution to the problem I'm facing. May it be a thought I've never had, a concept I've never considered, or an idea outside my own thought patterns."*

SKEPTIC'S CHALLENGE/ PRAYER: If it is true that there is no earthly problem that God does not have a heavenly solution for, where could you use wisdom today? Let's assume God has a great solution for the problem you need to solve. Maybe your simple prayer, even as a skeptic could be, *"God, please give me a complete or even partial solution to the problem I'm facing."* Maybe God will give you a thought you've never had, a concept you've never considered, or an idea outside your own thought patterns.

NOTES

WEEK TWO / DAY THREE

GOD IS OMNIPOTENT

7 "Can you fathom the mysteries of God?
  Can you probe the limits of the Almighty?
8 They are higher than the heavens above—what can you do?
  They are deeper than the depths below—what can you know?
9 Their measure is longer than the earth
  and wider than the sea.
10 If he comes along and confines you in prison
  and convenes a court, who can oppose him?
11 Surely he recognizes deceivers;
  and when he sees evil, does he not take note?"
JOB 11:7-11

"Now all glory to God, who is able, through his mighty power at work within us, to accomplish infinitely more than we might ask or think."
EPHESIANS 3:20 (NLT)

Omnipotent means to have unlimited power (omni = all; potent = powerful). God is able and powerful to do anything he wills without any effort on His part.

In our world, money can buy a lot. But there are also many things it can't buy. It can't buy more time, it can't buy love, it can't buy a cure, it can't buy happiness, it can't buy peace, it can't buy patience, and I could go on and on. There are all these things that only a divine power not of this world might be able to potentially touch.

In fact, in scripture we see God's power show up and provide people with all these things: more time (when Lazarus is resurrected), a cure (when the blind man is healed), peace, patience, and other things only a divine power can give.

I'm sure if you're like me, there are places in your life where outside of some divine power, nothing you do can make a real difference.

And yet Ephesians 3:20 (NLT) says, "Now all glory to God, who is able, through his mighty power at work within us, to accomplish infinitely more than we might ask or think."

God is able through His power to work within us to accomplish more things than we might ask or even think of. So asking to see this type of power at work within us should be something we pursue.

You might be thinking, if this type of divine power is meant to be at work in every Christian, then why don't we see God's magnificent power at work all the time?

James 4:2 might give us an answer to that. He says, "… you do not have because you do not ask God."

I would argue the majority of Christians simply do not ask with faith and then wait for His power to be seen.

Picture it this way. Let's say my six-year-old asks for a peanut butter and jelly sandwich. I reply by saying, "Sure thing, just give me a minute." In his haste and lack of patience he decides he is not willing to wait the minute, so he makes the sandwich himself. Now because he's a six-year-old, with six-year-old hands and six-year-old skills, the peanut butter ends up not being layered smoothly on the bread, the bread starts to break apart, and he puts on way too much jelly. As he sits there eating the sandwich he made, he starts to whine that the jelly is squishing out, the bread is breaking apart in his hands, and the peanut butter is too thick on one half of the sandwich.

It's not that he didn't ask me for help, it's that he didn't wait for me to do it for him. Way too often we do the same thing. We ask God to work in some powerful way in our lives. But before we wait a minute for Him to show up and show off, we immediately go to work doing it for ourselves. We try to handle it by our own strength and by our own power.

Now God is not our personal genie. Sometimes, where and how we want to see His power displayed is just not in line with God's plan. However, more often than not, I do believe God wants to work powerfully in our lives and we simply miss it.

God is powerful. God is able. God is big enough. God is strong enough. I believe God wants to display a divine and heavenly expression of His power in your life today.

DAILY DISCOVERY: What can money not buy in your life? We all have areas in our lives that outside of God's divine power, seem pretty hopeless. Yet God is all-powerful and He is able to do in our lives more than we could ask or think. Today, believe big for God to show His divine power in your life.

SKEPTIC'S CHALLENGE/ PRAYER: Pray this simple prayer: *"God, if you are real, show your power today to me in a real and tangible way."* Now wait and watch!

NOTES

WEEK TWO / DAY FOUR

GOD IS OMNIPRESENT

7 "Where can I go from Your Spirit?
   Where can I flee from your presence?
8 If I go up to the heavens, you are there;
   if I make my bed in the depths, you are there.
9 If I rise on the wings of the dawn,
   if I settle on the far side of the sea,
10 even there your hand will guide me,
   your right hand will hold me fast."

PSALM 139:7-10

"'Am I a God at hand,' declares the LORD, 'and not a God far away? Can a man hide himself in secret places so that I cannot see him?' declares the LORD 'Do I not fill heaven and earth?' declares the LORD."

JEREMIAH 23:23-24 (ESV)

With nine children, my wife and I are rarely alone. When they were younger we used to at least get a couple of hours together once we put them to bed, but the older they have gotten, the harder it has become to find alone time as a couple or as individuals.

The irony is that someday when they all grow up and move out, I will likely long for the hectic nature and constant hustle and bustle we've always had around the house. But for right now, I just want some alone time. (There are probably hundreds of moms and dads of young kids who are shouting "Amen" to that.)

The interesting thing about proximity to people, is that being around people doesn't always equate to feeling like you are "with" them. Have you ever heard the phrase, "Alone in a crowd?" I've seen it hundreds of times in youth ministry: there's a crowd of kids, while one stands alone off to the side. And unless we go and purposely reach out to that kid, he or she may leave feeling like they were completely alone.

I have felt that way in life. In proximity to many, yet feeling all alone. Maybe you have, too.

The awesome thing about this character trait of God is that it addresses and brings hope to our loneliness.

It also brings accountability to our actions. If God is everywhere at all times, it also means He is present in our stupidity. He was there when you went to that place you know you shouldn't have gone, or did that thing you know you shouldn't have done. I don't say that as a threat. More than anything I'm constantly enamored by the fact that God still loves me, forgives me, and is good to me in spite of the fact that He was with me while I was being a fool.

But His presence with me is always less of a threat and more of a comfort.

Not long ago I took some of my own kids caving. When I say caving, this is not one of those caves with paved paths and pre-lit colored scenes filled with stalagmites and stalactites. No, this is a get-down-and-dirty-and-crawl-on-your-belly-in-the-mud type cave. It's also a cave with hundreds of tiny crevices, and nooks and crannies, each one looking as if it could lead to another space to explore. It had been nearly 20 years since I had been in this particular cave and all I remembered was that there were a few specific tiny crevices I was going to have to find to get through the cave. To save time, on multiple occasions I told my kids to stay put while I explored ahead to make sure I wasn't leading them down a long dead end. During one of these mini-explorations I found myself further and further away from my kids. I kept going through tiny holes, believing I was going in the right direction, yet not seeing any sign that this was leading me where I wanted to go. About five minutes into this exploration I had gotten so far I couldn't hear my kids' voices, I couldn't even remember where I came from, and I was feeling very alone. It was at this moment that Psalm 139 came rushing to the forefront of my mind. "If I make my bed in the depths, You are there." And in the darkness of the cave I prayed a simple prayer. "God, you are with me, help me to know you are with me." Immediately a comfort came over my heart that I can only describe as an awareness of His presence with me. I literally felt as if I were following someone through the cave. And yes, moments later, I found my way through, eventually got back to my kids, and led them through the rest of the cave.

Perhaps you feel alone in life. All of us will face some days where we will feel like no one sees us, no one understands us, no one gets us, no one is with us... and we feel alone. I believe one of the devil's greatest tricks is getting us to believe the lie that we are alone and on our own.

If God is always with you it would make sense that the enemy would tell you the opposite. But what I've discovered is that God is always with me and if I slow down and look for His presence, I find Him every time. I've seen Him clear as day, on a mountain top in Alaska, in the northwoods of Wisconsin, on the shores of a lake that is smooth as glass early in the morning, and in the darkness of a cave. I have also seen Him and known His presence on the drive to work, while lying on the floor in my son's room as I lay him down for bed at night, while mowing the lawn, and while sitting on my front porch. He meets me in the extraordinary and in the completely ordinary places of my life. I invite you to discover our omnipresent God today.

DAILY DISCOVERY: Where do you feel alone? Maybe it's in a decision you have to make or in a struggle you hope to overcome. Maybe it's a very literal reality where you live alone and often feel very alone. Today let's look for every place God is with us. Keep your eyes open and heart sensitive to His presence being with you throughout the day.

SKEPTIC'S CHALLENGE/ PRAYER: *"God, please remind me today of a time you were with me when I felt all alone and please help me to know you are present with me today."*

WEEK TWO / DAY FIVE

GOD IS OMNISCIENT

"Remember the former things, those of long ago;
    I am God, and there is no other;
    I am God, and there is none like me.
I make known the end from the beginning,
    from ancient times, what is still to come.
I say, 'My purpose will stand,
    and I will do all that I please.'"

ISAIAH 46:9-10

Omniscience is all knowing. A.W. Tozer writes this about God's omniscience: "God perfectly knows Himself and, being the source and author of all things, it follows that He knows all that can be known. And this He knows instantly and with a fullness of perfection that includes every possible item of knowledge concerning everything that exists or could have existed anywhere in the universe at any time in the past or that may exist in the centuries or ages yet unborn."

In the 2000 movie "What Women Want," Mel Gibson plays an advertising director who is responsible for coming up with marketing ideas for a series of feminine products. He wakes up the next morning with the ability to hear every thought of every woman he is in proximity to. Of course, in this comedy he goes on to use and sometimes misuse this new-found ability.

How would you like that? Someone else knowing every thought you've ever had.

Not only is God with you always as we considered yesterday, He also knows everything about you. He knows your every thought, He knows your every fear, He knows your intentions, your hopes, your dreams, your desires, everything. He also knows your every hurt, every pain, every tear you've cried, every let-down you've experienced, and every heartbreak you've had.

He knows every smirk you've made, every laugh you've laughed, every ounce of joy you've experienced… He knows it all. Every high. Every low.

He knows the number of hairs on your head, or in my case, how many hairs I'll lose. He knows how many scraped knees I'll have, how many concussions I'll experience, how many stitches I'll get, how many broken bones I'll have. (You're probably thinking, "How reckless is this guy, naming all these injuries?" And you would be right.)

The point is simple. He knows it all.

Have you ever tried to withhold information from God in a prayer? If you're not a praying person then maybe not, but if you are, then you probably have. It works like this. You really want a new car, but don't want to sound selfish to God, so you ask for some means of transportation. As if He won't know what your heart's desire is. He totally knows you want a car, so just say it. Or, you're having major doubts in your faith, but you don't want Him to know, so you pray a prayer that sounds full of faith. How silly is that? God knows your heart, He knows your thoughts, and He is going to love you in spite of them, but it does you no good to pretend that you're keeping Him safe from knowing all that you're thinking.

One of the sweetest things is knowing that He loves me in spite of my thoughts, in spite of what I've done in the past or will do in the future.

Because He is all knowing, the greatest thing that goes with that is that He knows specifically and exactly what is significant to us.

For example, if there is a number that is significant to you, a color, a place, a memory, a sports team, a symbol, anything: He knows it. And the upside of Him knowing it is that there are endless ways throughout the day for God to drop sweet, yet significant, personalized things that only He and you know, into your day.

One of my favorite restaurants is Chili's. I'm a sucker for their chips and salsa and fajitas. But eating out can add up and I can't afford to eat there too often. God knows how much I love Chili's, but He also knows the cost of dining out, and so for a few years God really showed off His love for my wife and I in a pretty bizarre way. One Christmas, Lisa and I were given a couple of gift cards to Chili's. This was exciting for us. Now, all we had to do was cover the babysitter. We planned the night, got the babysitter, grabbed our gift cards, and went out for a great meal. However, when it came time to pay the bill, our server walked over and said, "Someone has already paid your bill, tip included." It was so strange, we had a gift card and we couldn't even use it. Well, that didn't just happen that one time. No, it continued to happen every time Lisa and I went to Chili's for more than three years. I remember the first time after years of this going on that the server came and just dropped off the bill. We were out of gift cards and I just kind of stared at it not knowing quite what to do. Lisa and I started looking around the restaurant, wanting to give ample time for anyone to pay our bill. I know it sounds crazy now, but we had gotten used to God showing His love and kindness to us in this significant gift that was very personalized to us.

That's how our omniscient God works. He knows you personally and knows exactly what you and I need (and even want).

DAILY DISCOVERY: Look for God today to show up in a way that only you would see or recognize. He knows your every need and every thought. What have you been pretending to hide from Him that you can honestly talk with Him about today?

SKEPTIC'S CHALLENGE/ PRAYER: *"God, since you know my every thought, here's what I'm really dealing with…*

And if you really know me personally, would you show me something that would only mean something significant to me?"

WEEK TWO / DAY SIX & SEVEN

DAY 6: LET THAT THOUGHT SIMMER

What idea was most challenging to you this week?

DAY 7: LET THAT THOUGHT SIMMER

What day from this week or concept do you want to rethink about?

NOTES

WEEK THREE

WEEK THREE / DAY ONE

GOD IS INFINITE

"He is before all things, and in him all things hold together."
COLOSSIANS 1:17

"Great is our LORD, and abundant in power;
  his understanding is beyond measure"
PSALM 147:5 (ESV)

To say that God is infinite is to say that he is self-existing and has always existed. Meaning, nothing created Him and He has no beginning and no end. He has been for all of time and will be for all of time.

I remember as a young child trying to think about God having no beginning and my head would start to hurt. Honestly, the same still happens today. It just feels impossible to understand. Even today as I think about the idea that God created us as eternal beings, I start to feel a little exhausted just thinking about it. If after this life, our souls spend eternity either with God or apart from Him, I always feel like it sounds a little exhausting just going on forever and ever.

Yet perhaps it's exhausting because we only understand time in linear fashion. We think through the lens of timelines and chronological dates, but what if God views time entirely differently?

Consider some of these verses:

"...he chose us... before the creation of the world..." **EPHESIANS 1:4**

"Before a word is on my tongue
  you, LORD, know it completely." **PSALM 139:4**

"Your eyes saw my unformed body;
  all the days ordained for me were written in your book
before one of them came to be." **PSALM 139:16**

"...With the LORD a day is like a thousand years, and a thousand years are like a day." 2 PETER 3:8b

I've used this illustration before. Let's imagine your life experiences painted on a piece of glass. Each experience gets painted onto its own pane. We would naturally put those panes into an order, one after another. And I imagine God sees them in order as well, but instead of placing them side by side, He stacks them one on top of each other in order. He can't help but view them all simultaneously and see them all one through the other. He can't help but see how one experience impacted another, how another helped shape and form character traits that would forever make you who you are. He also can't help but see you as a finished product of heaven.

For Christians, He sees them complete, lacking nothing, without pain, without sorrow or tears, victorious.

My son got his driving permit yesterday. That means in six months he will be able to get his official license and hit the roads as a full fledged driver. Watch out, folks. While it hasn't happened yet, I can already imagine it and picture it in my mind almost as clear as day. My son will walk in the house, a slight grin on his face. He'll probably try to pull a fast one on me and initially tell me that he failed his road test, then a few seconds later, he'll burst into laughter and say, "No, I passed." I'll say, "Buddy, way to go, I'm so proud of you."

Now, I'm not calling myself psychic or anything, it's just how I can imagine it playing out and it will be here before I know it. The difference with God is instead of imagining it, He sees it. He is fully present in this moment of your life right now as you read these words and yet He sees your yesterday in the same clarity and brilliance as He also sees your tomorrow. To Him, they overlap and play together to make you who you are. And everything He can accomplish in your life, He sees that as well.

My oldest son is an amazing musician. He plays the drums and guitar, and is a talented singer. He writes his own songs and I'm not just playing the proud parent card, he's legitimately quite good. He's now in college, getting a degree in music with a vocal emphasis and it's hard to imagine him not being an amazing musician. But I remember years ago when all he was doing was drumming and he was only okay at best. We were driving out to Montana as a family. That's a 24-hour drive in the car. All I can say is 24 hours in the car provides a lot of thinking time. During that thinking time, I'm thinking about my kids, I'm talking with God in my head, and I feel like God tells me to invest in my son. He had been starting to play around on some of my older guitars that I have sitting around the house and I felt like I could see the potential in him. So I talked it over with my wife and we presented him with an opportunity. I told him I wanted to invest in him toward a guitar and whatever he was willing to put toward it with his own money, my wife and I would match it. When we got home from that trip we went out and bought his first guitar together. And the rest, as they say, is history… at least his history, so far.

If God is outside of time, then He sees a decision that you will make today and how it will become a critical part of your story tomorrow. He sees how your first guitar can set you on a path to becoming a great musician. He sees how your creative mind is setting you up to bring wonder into the world. He sees how your leadership bent is setting you up to impact and influence so many others. He sees how your painful circumstance today will become a part of someone else's healing process next year or in the years to come. He can't help but see the whole story and how it works together, plays together, and interacts together. He can't help but see the finished product from the parts. And He can't help but see your successes that come from risk, hard work, and many failures along the way.

God, the infinite one, is entangled in your story from start to finish. Perhaps the best part is reminding our hearts what Philippians 1:6 says: "… he who began a good work in you will carry it on to completion…" **That He who is outside of time works in our lives within time, to complete us for all of time.**

DAILY DISCOVERY: Think back to one small thing that impacted your life in a huge way. Ask God to do it again and this time for a God-sized impact. What small decision can you make today, or investment can you start sowing into that God can use for an impact for tomorrow?

SKEPTIC'S CHALLENGE/ PRAYER: *"God, if you know my whole story, help me to see one piece of my story today through the lens of how you see it. How were you entangled in my story years ago that has impacted where I am today?"*

NOTES

WEEK THREE / DAY TWO

GOD IS SELF-SUFFICIENT

"For as the Father has life in himself, so he has granted the Son also to have life in himself."

JOHN 5:26

As a parent of nine, I've watched kids become self-sufficient time and time again. There are a ton of these milestones that as kids pass, make it easier for the parents along the way. Some of the greatest are when they can feed themselves, dress themselves, bathe themselves, pick out their own clothes, pick up after themselves, read to themselves, do their homework without help, and the list goes on and on. Each one of these independent mile markers is a reminder that they don't have to get what they need from me anymore.

God is completely self-sufficient. And as pastor and author Tim Temple writes, "God is perfectly complete within his own being."

What self-sufficiency does is it satisfies those personal needs. When a child feeds themselves they are satisfying that need for themselves. When they dress themselves, they are satisfying that need for themselves, and so forth. And because God is self-sufficient, we can go to Him to satisfy all our needs.

Even though we grow in our self-sufficiency as we mature and become adults, in our humanity we are creatures still in need of a satisfaction that can only come from outside ourselves. There is an entire book of the Bible dedicated to this discovery: Ecclesiastes. It was written by King Solomon who pursued finding satisfaction in all the things of this world. He looked for satisfaction in work, in worldly pleasures, in wealth, in food, in wisdom, and in the end he called the pursuit folly.

At the end of it all, in the second to last verse of the book Solomon says, "...here is the conclusion of the matter: Fear God and keep his commandments, for this is the whole duty of man," (Ecclesiastes 12:13). The word that gets translated as *fear* can also be translated as *to live in awe of*. This is not about being literally afraid, but instead it is about living our lives awestruck by the awesomeness of God. There is something about the awesomeness of God, His presence, and following His ways that actually satisfies our hungry souls.

Years ago I remember seeing a video clip from the summer Olympics in Rio. In it, U.S. pole vaulter and Army reservist Sam Kendricks stopped mid-run to stand at attention for the national anthem. In the video you hear the national anthem start and immediately see him come to a screeching halt and then his eyes start searching for the American flag. He stands at attention for the entirety of the national anthem and then immediately when it is finished, he picks up his pole and continues his vault. This is a great picture of what this Biblical word of fear looks like: it's awe that causes everything to stop and come to attention. Sam Kendricks is not afraid of the national anthem, nor the American flag, but instead he has such reverence for them that everything must stop and realign around them for that moment. In the same way, the satisfaction that our souls long for will never be found in anything from this world. It will only be found when our lives pause (and we stop for a moment and stop chasing after the things of this world) and our attention is focused on the only One who can satisfy our every need.

DAILY DISCOVERY: Let's assume God is ready to bring great satisfaction to you today. Where do you need it? Where are you currently looking to find it? Where does your life need to come to a screeching halt so you can focus your eyes on the one who can bring real satisfaction?

SKEPTIC'S CHALLENGE/ PRAYER: *"God, I have never found satisfaction in_____.*

Could you show me a glimpse of satisfaction from you in this area?"

WEEK THREE / DAY THREE

GOD IS JUST

"The Rock, his work is perfect,

for all his ways are justice.

A God of faithfulness and without iniquity,

just and upright is he."

DEUTERONOMY 32:4 (ESV)

What does it mean that God is just? It means more than he is simply fair. It means he always does what is right and good toward all men.

One of the most common statements I hear from my kids when I tell them what they can't do is "so-and-so did it." One kid sneaks a cookie and then all the others believe the just and right thing is for them to all be able to sneak a cookie. As a parent, I fully know that my kids are experiencing different standards over the years. My oldest kids were always in bed on time when they were younger, while my younger kids constantly get away with staying up later. One could argue that it's not fair and they would probably be right.

I'm grateful that God is not like me. He is fair and just with all of His children. Sometimes his justice seems like it is slow in coming, but justice will be brought to everything in time.

Have you ever been wronged and you are just waiting and waiting for justice? For the past couple of years my wife and I were incorrectly billed for something. When we recently realized it, I contacted the company and started the process to hopefully be refunded. Because it added up to a significant amount of money over such a long period of time, a special claim had to be submitted. In this case it was the company's mistake and morally I believe they should have to reimburse us, however, we shall see if justice ever comes to us.

For now, it's just kind of lingering out there. There is no resolution to the injustice. The wrong has not yet been righted.

Because it's not your money in limbo, you probably don't feel the tension I do. But we can all relate to the innate longing to see justice brought to unfair situations.

Spiritually speaking, there will be a righting of all that is broken and wrong in this world. According to the book of Revelation, there will be resolution and there will be an end to all evil. And while I love how that sounds, one of the most spiritually ironic truths for Christians is that we totally do not receive what we deserve. We truly do not get treated justly for what we have done.

I talked about this when we addressed mercy. Our sins deserved punishment and yet Christ took all our punishment upon himself at the cross. If there was ever a person who was not treated fairly, it was Jesus. He, who was perfect and deserved no punishment, took all our punishment upon Himself. Yet He did it willingly to make a way to have a relationship with you and me.

But it's not always about fairness, it's about rightness. He did bring justice to our wrongs, a payment for sin was paid… but it was not paid by us, it was paid by Jesus. Rightness was accomplished. He did something that was completely right and completely good. This is the work of our just God.

DAILY DISCOVERY: God is so just. He is completely right and completely good. Where in your life were things unfair? Ask God today to show you how He is bringing or will bring justice to those situations.

SKEPTIC'S CHALLENGE/ PRAYER: *"God, I probably haven't gotten what I deserve in life. Show me where you've been merciful to me. And give me a glimpse of your character of justice where you will bring justice to all the wrong that has been done to me in my life."*

WEEK THREE / DAY FOUR

GOD IS IMMUTABLE

Pastor Sam Storms writes this about the good news of God's unchanging nature: "What all this means, very simply, is that God is dependable! Our trust in him is therefore a confident trust, for we know that he will not, indeed cannot, change. His purposes are unfailing, his promises unassailable. It is because the God who promised us eternal life is immutable that we may rest assured that nothing, not trouble or hardship or persecution or famine or nakedness or danger or sword shall separate us from the love of Christ. It is because Jesus Christ is the same yesterday, today, and forever that neither angels nor demons, neither the present nor the future, not even powers, height, depth, nor anything else in all creation, will be able to separate us from the love of God that is in Christ Jesus our LORD (Romans 8:35-39)!"

I grew up going on vacation every year to Eagle River, Wisconsin. We would rent a cabin on a lake and spend the week waterskiing, tubing, and playing. Inevitably, every year, there is a day where the temps stay cooler and it rains off and on. It's on that day we would go to town. We never wanted to waste a beautiful afternoon when we could be skiing on the lake, so we would watch the weather forecast and try to predict and plan which day would end up being our shopping day.

Downtown is nothing spectacular. In truth you can walk all of it in probably 20 minutes. It's a typical small town tourist setting. There are a couple of traditional corner stores, T-shirt shops, souvenir shops, candy and ice cream shops. What is amazing is that 40 years later, I take my kids to those same shops and they all look almost identical to how they did when I was young. They still sell a lot of the exact same merchandise. The colors are the same, the set up is the same, the carpets look the same, and they even smell the same. It's like they are caught in time, and there is great comfort in the certainty of the sameness that this small town offers year after year.

While we might call those shops stalled out or dated, God is not stalled out nor dated. But He is the same yesterday, today, and forever. I actually find great comfort in that. If that's true, then the way God treated and interacted with His chosen nation Israel, the way He worked through His prophets and led His kings, the way Jesus treated sinners and rejects is still the way He treats us.

One of the statements that I consider to be a compliment is when people say about me, "Josh is the same person on and off the stage. What you see up there is what you get here as well."

What can sometimes happen is we start to think God interacted with His people back in the Bible one way and He interacts with us today another way. But, just like I'm the same on and off the stage, the God of the Bible is the God of today. And the way God interacted with His people in the Bible is still the way God interacts with us today. He is the same.

One of the exercises that I do regularly is imagine myself in the stories I read from the Bible. I read of God speaking to Joshua in the Old Testament, "Be strong and courageous," and I imagine God saying the same thing to me today. I imagine Jesus reinstating Peter to ministry after Peter abandoned Him and denied Him during His crucifixion and I imagine Jesus saying the same words to me when I've blown it, with compassion in His smile and a belief in me in His gaze. Maybe my imagination gets away from me at times, but I just can't help it, knowing He is the same yesterday, today, and forever.

DAILY DISCOVERY: Ask God to bring a Bible story to your mind today. If you were the character in that story, what was our God of the past, who is also the God of our present, doing or saying to that individual and what might He be saying to you today?

SKEPTIC'S CHALLENGE/ PRAYER: Did you ever hear a Bible story that seemed to impress you? Or a Bible character that impressed you? What was God doing then? *"God, if you are the same, yesterday, today, and forever, what are you still wanting to say to your children today?"*

NOTES

WEEK THREE / DAY FIVE

GOD IS GLORIOUS

"... but indeed as I live, all the earth will be filled with the glory of the
LORD."

NUMBERS 14:21 (AMP)

"And blessed be His glorious name forever;
And may the whole earth be filled with His glory.
Amen, and Amen."

PSALM 72:19

The Hebrew word that is used for *glory* in the Old Testament has the
simple meaning of "heaviness" or "weight." It was used to express
the ideas of importance, greatness, honor, splendor, power, and so on.

Glory is interesting. It's something that you can have but it is also
something you can give.

You may see a magnificent sunset and say, "That is glorious." Or you may
rave about your favorite sports team in which case you are directing or
bestowing glory upon them.

God is glorious in the display of His greatness and He also receives glory
when it is directed to Him because of His greatness.

When Jesus is born the angels appear to the shepherds and scripture says,
"The glory of the LORD shone about them," then it goes on to say that
they start declaring, "Glory to God in the highest and on earth peace to
whom His favor rests." So they themselves are experiencing God's glory
and the angels are declaring God is glorious and giving glory to God.

But regardless of whether glory is being experienced or glory is being
given, it is all driven by the "heaviness" or "weight" or "greatness" that

is being experienced because of God. The presence of God and His handiwork causes a heaviness or weight to be impressed upon our hearts.

Ask yourself this question: have you ever been speechless due to something wonderful? Maybe something that causes delight and awe. I think of a sunrise or a sunset, the birth of a child, holding a child for the first time and seeing an entire life resting in your hands, the changing of the autumn leaves, the frost covered trees in winter, a wind that can blow you over, or the stillness of a star-filled night, a perfectly timed hug, or a song sung with what I would imagine to be angelic grace or beauty.

Each of these cause a heaviness to overwhelm my soul. It's this heaviness that is the glory of God. It's in this moment that we are experiencing what the Bible talks about when it says, "The whole earth is filled with His glory."

God Himself and His works are constantly on display, causing people everywhere to stop and take notice. You realize, right now someone on the planet is having a breathtaking moment where they are overwhelmed by the heaviness of the greatness of God. They may not realize it is God, or even give Him glory, but they are astounded by His glory all the same… and perhaps even the very words "That's glorious" may be slipping off their tongue.

DAILY DISCOVERY: The greatness of God is on constant display. This greatness causes a heaviness and weight upon the soul. Perhaps you see it daily, but look past it quickly in our distracted culture. Today look for the glory of God all around you. Look for His handiwork everywhere. Perhaps you will see the glory of God in more places than you ever imagine, as the whole earth is filled with His glory.

SKEPTIC'S CHALLENGE/ PRAYER: *"God, take my breath away today. Bring a weightiness to a moment in my day that causes me to take pause and be astounded."*

WEEK THREE / DAY SIX & SEVEN

DAY 6: LET THAT THOUGHT SIMMER

What idea was most challenging to you this week?

DAY 7: LET THAT THOUGHT SIMMER

What day from this week or concept do you want to rethink about?

WEEK FOUR

WEEK FOUR / DAY ONE

GOD IS RELENTLESS

"Now the tax collectors and sinners were all gathering around to hear Jesus. 2 But the Pharisees and the teachers of the law muttered, 'This man welcomes sinners and eats with them.'

3 Then Jesus told them this parable: 4 'Suppose one of you has a hundred sheep and loses one of them. Doesn't he leave the ninety-nine in the open country and go after the lost sheep until he finds it? 5 And when he finds it, he joyfully puts it on his shoulders 6 and goes home. Then he calls his friends and neighbors together and says, 'Rejoice with me; I have found my lost sheep.' 7 I tell you that in the same way there will be more rejoicing in heaven over one sinner who repents than over ninety-nine righteous persons who do not need to repent.'"

LUKE 15:1-7

I remember when Lisa and I started dating. We were students at Moody Bible Institute in downtown Chicago. As a conservative Bible college, it had what I consider to be a few strict rules. Looking back, they were probably great for me, but at the time I'm sure I loathed them. One that I hated most was our midnight curfew, especially in a season of dating and falling in love. In those first years of our relationship, I remember staying with Lisa till the last minute of every day. I would drop her off at the entrance to her building at 11:59 p.m. and sprint to my dormitory to make it in the front door by midnight. I literally wanted to soak up every minute in the presence of Lisa. I was in a season of constant pursuit of her. Every day seemed too short and every minute and opportunity to know her more or simply sit in her presence was not enough.

I imagine that's the type of pursuit God has for us constantly in our lives. In Luke 15, Jesus finds Himself in an interesting situation. He's breaking all the social rules of the day by hanging out with tax collectors and others that would have been labeled as sinners. In that day and age it was something good church-going people didn't do. But Jesus came to demolish every human tradition that pushed against the heart of God... and boy did Jesus do a good job of it.

In this encounter the religious leaders are gossiping and muttering about Jesus and who is hanging out with Him, and Jesus responds with a parable, which is a story that teaches a principle. In this case, Jesus talks about a wandering sheep and a shepherd who will leave 99 others to chase after the one. Once he finds the one, he celebrates with his friends that the one that was lost has been found.

In the same way, God is pursuing you. He'll do anything to get your attention. He's chasing after you till 11:59 p.m. each night. He's leaving the 99, which may seem a little irresponsible, to get the one.

In many ways that's how I see God's relentlessness. It seems irresponsible, irrational, illogical, and not like something God would do. But Jesus tells the story to illustrate a point, and the point is that this is exactly what God does to pursue us.

Cory Asbury wrote a song about this parable and in describing what motivated him to write his song, he described God's pursuit of us this way: "He is utterly unconcerned with the consequences of His actions with regards to His own safety, comfort, and well-being. His love isn't crafty or slick. It's not cunning or shrewd. In fact, all things considered, it's quite childlike, and might I even suggest, sometimes downright ridiculous. His love bankrupted heaven for you, for me. His love doesn't consider Himself first. It isn't selfish or self-serving. He doesn't wonder what He'll gain or lose by putting Himself on the line. He simply puts Himself out there on the off chance that you and I might look back at Him and give him that love in return."*

I've been a Christian for nearly 40 years, and the crazy thing is I feel like God is still pursuing me like day one. My heart still has times when it wanders. My attention is often drawn away from Him. My love is often divided. And yet, like an early dating relationship, God is doing all that He can to get our attention and affection and give His.

I still love my wife like those early days of dating… probably actually more so. Like a fine wine, time makes it richer. I feel the same, my love for Lisa is just richer and sweeter and more precious to me with every passing year. I still think about her constantly throughout my day and there will be times I do things for her that she may never even recognize, but I do it with her in mind. It may be making the bed, washing the dishes, getting her car washed and fueled up, taking out the trash, doing that 10 minute project she asked me to do or folding the laundry. Now before I make myself sound like Superman, these are some of the things I could and sometimes do, but the point is this: sometimes I do them simply thinking about her, loving her, wanting to dote on her, wanting to show her affection. It doesn't take much to miss it or just look past it. If she's had a busy day where she's been running a hundred miles an hour, I won't be mad if at the end of the day she doesn't recognize that I did some of those things for her. But it doesn't change the fact that I did that for her, with her in mind, to show my love and affection to her.

God is the same. Daily He is doing things in our lives to show His love and affection toward us. Unfortunately, many of us are also living our lives at a breakneck speed and we often just miss the small and subtle, yet special and specific displays of affection and pursuit God is doing in our lives.

Every time I've kept my eyes open looking for the pursuit of God in my life I see it. In fact I see it so often, it makes me wonder just how much God is pursuing all of mankind and if we just overlook it in our distracted world.

*Quote from Cory Asbury is from his video singing "Reckless Love" at Heaven Come Conference 2017 and is reprinted with permission from Bethel Music.

DAILY DISCOVERY: Let's take it to the extreme. Look for God's relentless pursuit of you today. Where is He making small and subtle, yet special and specific displays of affection in your life today?

SKEPTIC'S CHALLENGE/ PRAYER: *"I may feel like I'm not worthy of pursuit. I may even wonder if you are a loving or pursuing God, however, if You are still pursuing, would You please not quit pursuing me. Help me to see where You are trying to give Your attention and affection to me today."*

NOTES

WEEK FOUR / DAY TWO

GOD IS LOVE - HIS LOVE GOES "ALL IN"

[9] "This is how God showed his love among us: He sent his one and only Son into the world that we might live through him. [10] This is love: not that we loved God, but that he loved us and sent his Son as an atoning sacrifice for our sins."

1 JOHN 4:9-10

"For God so loved the world that he gave his one and only Son, that whoever believes in him shall not perish but have eternal life."

JOHN 3:16

I grew up in a poker-playing family. Not that we ever bet real money; our poker chips instead represented back rub time. And at the end of the night we would cash in our chips for a back rub from another family member. Now that I have kids of my own, we also play periodically and I think I've overlooked this important representation of what our chips could be traded in for. We don't cash in our chips for anything. As a result, my kids will periodically go "all in" with nothing really at stake. And when they lose all their chips in the game, there are no ramifications for their actions. In fact, we will usually give them some chips back to be able to keep playing.

God's love is such an "all in" action. He pushes in all His chips and bets the farm on His relationship with humanity. God's love is so significant that we're going to spend a few days just going to the extreme in processing His love.

I mentioned Cory Asbury yesterday. He continues to say about God's love: "His love isn't cautious, it's a love that sent His own son to die a gruesome death on a cross. There's no plan B with the love of God. He gives his heart so completely, so preposterously, that if refused, we would think it irreparably broken. Yet He gives himself away, again and again and again ... His love saw you when you hated Him, and all logic said, they'll reject me ... He said ... I lay my life on the line ..."*

I'm sure we've all known of someone in our life whose family member was diagnosed with cancer or some other terminal illness. There is nothing like it that will align priorities on heaven and earth in a matter of moments. I've heard many times over one of those individuals saying, "I would trade anything for a cure, I would trade all that I had for more time, I would do anything for the person I love." Ultimately, what is being seen is the value of a relationship. We would do anything for the relationship.

God sees us the same way. Our souls were in a downward spiral toward death and a broken relationship with our Heavenly Father. To save us and save the relationship, God displayed that same level of love toward us that He would go "all in" and give all He was able to give for us. He gave His one and only Son to lay down His life for us at the cross.

I love 1 John 4:9-10, which blatantly gives us a definition of love. He says, "this is love:" and what follows is God's perfect definition and picture of love. He goes on to say, here it is: He loved us and sent His Son. This gift of Jesus coming, dwelling among mankind, laying down His life for us and for our sins, and offering us new life through faith in Him is the greatest display of love in all of history.

So today would you consider God's love through the lens of sacrifice and going "all in?" God only had one way of displaying His love and it was by going "all in" for us.

DAILY DISCOVERY: Today, take your faith to the extreme and let's assume that God's love is an "all in" love for us. How does it impact your love in return? How does it impact your perspective of love in general? Where is God going to wow you today with a display of His "all in" type of love?

SKEPTIC'S CHALLENGE/ PRAYER: *"If you really love me with this "all in" type of love, help me to see it, or know it, or wrap my head around it in a fresh way or for the first time."*

*Quote from Cory Asbury is from his video singing "Reckless Love" at Heaven Come Conference 2017 and is reprinted with permission from Bethel Music.

WEEK FOUR / DAY THREE

GOD IS LOVE - HIS LOVE IS UNENDING

37 "No, in all these things we are more than conquerors through him who loved us. 38 For I am convinced that neither death nor life, neither angels nor demons, neither the present nor the future, nor any powers, 39 neither height nor depth, nor anything else in all creation, will be able to separate us from the love of God that is in Christ Jesus our LORD."

ROMANS 8:37-39

I'm sure there is no subject that gets more attention than the subject of love. Songs are written about it; poems try to capture the fullness of it in sonnet and rhyme; movies, books, and stories are written about it; dates and romantic gestures are designed around it; people live for it—to know it, to experience it. It's expressed in a rose, a lyric, a gentle touch, a gaze, a wink, or a smile. Words and phrases try their best to capture it, actions try to display it, and hearts try to fully experience it.

There is confusion in our culture today around love; that love equals approval. Or that unconditional love equals unconditional acceptance or approval. As parents we know this is not true. I don't have to approve of my children's actions to still love them. In fact I can strongly oppose their decisions, their beliefs, or their actions and still maintain a strong and consistent love for them. I believe we as parents get that trait from God. He too, can oppose our decisions, beliefs, or actions and yet maintain a strong and consistent love for us.

We have to wrap our minds around this reality because so often our love comes off as conditional. Throughout our lives we receive positive affirmation for positive behavior. When we get an A on a test our parents praise us. When we score our first goal our parents cheer us on, and so on. We naturally experience positive reinforcements for positive behavior. Conversely, we also experience negative reinforcement when we display negative behavior. If we tease our friend or sibling or do poorly on a test, we receive a negative response from our parents. No parents cheer their child on for an F. So even though they may love us unconditionally, sometimes the love feels more conditional than it is.

Sometimes we project that upon our Heavenly Father. We do something that we instinctively know is wrong or hurtful to others and thus is wrong and hurtful toward our relationship with God, and we assume He will withhold love for us or be mad at us. While God does not approve of sinful behavior, nor could He as He is holy, His love for us is undiminished and unshaken.

I've heard way too many times people say, "I get that God loves me, but you don't know what I've done." It's like they are saying, "I understand that God loves everyone, but I'm the exception to the rule, at least around this one thing that I've done. God will love everyone else unconditionally, but with me, conditions must be applied."

But it's just not true.

In Romans it says that nothing "in all creation, will be able to separate us from the love of God that is in Christ Jesus our LORD."

All of creation is a whole lot of everything. It sounds like we could get pretty creative in our recklessness and still not be able to outrun, outlast, or outlive God's love for us. Not that it is the goal. It is not. We would consider it a pretty messed up relationship with anyone here on earth if you made it your goal to offend and hurt them as often as you could knowing they would love you unconditionally. Yet God will love you that relentlessly even if we live that way.

There is absolutely nothing we can do to escape the love of God.

DAILY DISCOVERY: Sometimes there are areas in our lives where we assume God's love will never reach. Like, God's love will never love "middle school Josh and all that happened in my life during those years" or "work Josh" or fill in the blank for a time in your life where you feel like His love for you would not have been natural. Maybe there are some places in your life now where you feel like His love is unable to reach. Take this to the extreme and let's declare over our lives that God loved and loves me in each of those seasons and occasions. There is no place, no sin, no behavior, and no belief that can separate me from the love of God. Write down how God changes your perspective of His love today.

SKEPTIC'S CHALLENGE/ PRAYER: Where or when have you assumed God did not love you? Pray this: *"God if you loved me through a season when I felt unlovable, help me to understand how You loved me then. Help me to see how You love me today even with my current belief about You."*

NOTES

WEEK FOUR / DAY FOUR

GOD IS LOVE - HIS LOVE IS ABUNDANTLY PATIENT

"But you, LORD, are a compassionate and gracious God,
   slow to anger, abounding in love and faithfulness."

PSALM 86:15

I've shared with you how my family is pretty serious about waterskiing. However, to have any success in any sport requires a lot of failure. In skiing it includes a lot of trying and a lot of falling. Part of the process of getting someone to ski for the first time usually includes countless tries. They drag behind the boat, they struggle to even keep their skis straight, and as soon as they yell, "Hit it!" they are falling over the tips of their skis and taking in a mouthful of water. Sounds fun, right? It is, once you get up. But until then, it's a lot of falling and dragging and near-drowning. We've done this sometimes for hours behind a boat trying to get someone up for their first time.

Even though they are falling, and even though they are failing constantly, we keep pulling and cheering and coaching until they get it. I'm not going to lie, sometimes it requires a lot of patience for the boat driver and those in the boat. But we are hopeful for the moment of success.

In my life as a child, as a parent, as a spouse, as an employer, as a friend, and as a follower of Jesus, I've fallen and failed more times than I would like to admit. I've blown it over and over again. And yet God's love for me has been so patient. He's like the boat driver who believes in you, is hoping for you, is coaching and cheering you on, and will patiently love you until you get it.

If you've ever struggled with an addiction or know someone who has, you've probably seen in them their own personal desire to get out of the mess they are caught in. Yet they continue to fail and fall to it over and over again. From an earthly and human perspective it is tough to stick with those relationships and believe for them that they will ever get out. But that's what Christ does for us. He believes you can get out, He made a way for you to get out, and He loves you all the way out of the mess you're in.

I'm so grateful He is slow to anger. I'm so grateful His love faithfully endures through my failures.

Hudson Taylor once said, "All God's giants were all weak men and women who got a hold of God's faithfulness."

That is God and that is His love. He is faithfully and patiently pulling the boat until you get up. He is slow to anger and faithfully loving you to the very end.

DAILY DISCOVERY: Let's take our faith to the extreme by believing God's love is patient and faithful. He is believing for you and with you, and He is cheering you on through every fall and every failure. Let's believe His love for you is not a consolation prize type of love, but it is fierce, it is the best, it is the strongest, and it is persevering with you to the very end.

SKEPTIC'S CHALLENGE/ PRAYER: Where would earthly love have already abandoned you? Let's consider that God's love is still with you and is patiently with you to the very end. *"God, help me to know Your love has never left me, through all my faults and all my failures, Your love is with me to the end."*

NOTES

WEEK FOUR / DAY FIVE

GOD IS THE RULER WHO DOESN'T FORCE HIS RULERSHIP

"After the earthquake came a fire, but the LORD was not in the fire. And after the fire came a gentle whisper."

1 KINGS 19:12

Have you ever met a gentle giant? There was a guy in my church who was a bodybuilder. I'm not talking about someone who was in good shape, or had some decent muscle. This guy had MUS-CLES! He was ginormous. He was probably six feet five inches tall and could bench over 600 pounds. He was a mean, lean, muscle machine. But at the same time, he was gentle as could be. If you didn't know him, you probably would have just steered clear, but those who knew him, knew there was nothing to steer clear of. He was kind, soft spoken; very much a gentle giant.

While God is infinite, all powerful, all knowing, everywhere at once, glorious, abundantly loving, merciful, and gracious, He at the same time is somewhat of a gentle giant. He is the lover who doesn't force us to love Him back. The Ruler who doesn't force us to follow His rules. The King who doesn't force us to acknowledge His kingship. The Almighty who approaches us like a gentle whisper.

The beauty of relationships is that a true relationship is based on choice. I chose my wife and she has chosen me back. This is what makes the love relationship so sweet. God chooses us and the bizarre and amazing thing is while He can do absolutely anything He wants, He allows us to choose. Choose obedience, choose love, choose Him back... otherwise it wouldn't be a real relationship. And He does it, not in a domineering way, but a gentle, sweet, and loving way.

There is an awesome moment in scripture when God's presence comes on display for the prophet Elijah. It's found in 1 Kings 19.

11 "The LORD said, 'Go out and stand on the mountain in the presence of the LORD, for the LORD is about to pass by.'
Then a great and powerful wind tore the mountains apart and shattered the rocks before the LORD, but the LORD was not in the wind. After the wind there was an earthquake, but the LORD was not in the earthquake. 12 After the earthquake came a fire, but the LORD was not in the fire. And after the fire came a gentle whisper." 1 KINGS 19:11-12

What's awesome about this moment is that God's power and presence had the ability to tear the mountain apart, shatter the rocks, shake the earth, and consume everything present with fire. In many ways, what God was doing was showing Elijah what He was capable of. This is how mighty and powerful God is; it's like God is showing Elijah all that His presence carries, but it is just a pre-show of His presence. Yet, when He arrives He's not this domineering force. Instead He came as "a gentle whisper."

This is who God is. He is all powerful, Lord of Lords and King of Kings, yet He is presenting Himself to humanity in a gentle, kind, and compassionate way. He comes to us not forcing Himself upon us, but instead gently allowing us to choose Him in return.

Did you ever have a crush on someone who didn't like you back? It's kind of heartbreaking, yet at the same time you wouldn't want the relationship if they genuinely didn't want you back. I wonder how God feels as He loves us so relentlessly and yet most of humanity doesn't reciprocate this love. He has all the power to make us love Him back, and yet chooses to allow us to choose Him.

This may be the most important thing God ever did for us. He gave us choice. He gave us a personality and a will. He gave us the ability to make our own decisions and allows us to live by our decisions.

He is the gentle giant, who could overwhelm us with His power and presence, but instead approaches us like a gentle whisper allowing us to choose Him back.

DAILY DISCOVERY: Let's take our faith to the extreme today. Where has God been so gentle with you? Is there a place in your life today where God is trying to give you a gentle nudge in the right direction? Look for the gentle and kind hand of God in your life today and expect Him to show up.

SKEPTIC'S CHALLENGE/ PRAYER: *"God, if you are real, thank you for giving me the choice to believe or not believe in You. Since You are gentle in Your relationships, help me to see or hear You today and recognize the places where You approach me like a gentle whisper."*

NOTES

WEEK FOUR / DAY SIX & SEVEN

DAY 6: LET THAT THOUGHT SIMMER

What idea was most challenging to you this week?

DAY 7: LET THAT THOUGHT SIMMER

What day from this week or concept do you want to rethink about?

NOTES

OUR IDENTITY - WHO HE SAYS WE ARE

INTRODUCTION TO PART TWO

We've taken the first four weeks to focus on the character traits of God. The reason why this is crucial is because, for the remainder of this God Experiment, we are going to be taking a deep dive into who He says we are. That foundation is critical, because by now, I hope you've gotten a glimpse into who He is as trustworthy, loving, gracious, merciful, faithful, good, etc.: God.

Have you ever had someone come up to you and offer their opinion to you, but without an invitation to do so and without relationship? I've had that quite a few times as someone who is often on a stage and in the public eye. When there is no relationship, there is no trust. I don't know their heart, I don't know them, and thus what they think about me carries no real weight. Conversely, if it is from a close friend who is sharing their thoughts about me, I'm highly likely to consider what they are saying and take it to heart.

God cannot help but carry all of His attributes into what He says is true of us. As such, I hope by now you know you can trust that what God is saying about you carries His love, faithfulness, and goodness into these declarations over you.

Most of these declarations of your identity are from the perspective of God over redeemed children of God. Meaning, these positions of your identity are God's greatest view of you as a follower of Him: as a Christian.

If you don't consider yourself a Christian, or perhaps would call yourself a flat out non-believer, atheist, agnostic, skeptic, or even a seeker, this God Experiment is still a worthy endeavor for you. It's worth evaluating the person that you are and your identity that forms your belief and behaviors. I would invite you to at least give God a fair shake in your life and consider whether you think He has an identity that is different or perhaps even better for you than what you currently are living in.

John 10:10 says, "The thief comes only to steal and kill and destroy; I have come that they may have life, and have it to the full."

The first part of the verse describes Satan's goal in your life. The second part of that verse describes God's heart for your life.

From a Christian and Biblical perspective, the Bible teaches that Satan is a liar, a thief, and like a roaring lion, he is looking for who he may devour.

I believe the Bible and I believe the enemy is looking to rob, kill, and destroy every good intention and hope that God has for your life and your identity. So as you approach the following days and weeks, please hear each one of these God-given perspectives over you and ask the question: have you experienced or seen these character traits in your life? Do they feel absent? Is it possible the enemy has taken from you that which God has always desired for you?

WEEK FIVE

WEEK FIVE / DAY ONE

THE INNER IMAGE:
WINNING PRIVATE BATTLES PRECEDES
WINNING PUBLIC BATTLES

"...Though our outer self is wasting away, our inner self is being renewed day by day."

2 CORINTHIANS 4:16 (ESV)

When I say your 'inner image' what I'm talking about is what you truly believe (inside) about yourself. What you believe about yourself determines more than you'd probably like to admit.

Proverbs 23:7 says, "For as he thinks within himself, so he is."

This simply means that what you think about yourself will always supersede and precede your behavior: your thinking will trump your behavior and lead it.

I remember not too long ago, it was evening and we were looking for a movie to watch as a family. As I was scrolling through Netflix to find a good family flick, I came upon a few older movies that I knew the kids hadn't seen before. I remembered them as being great movies and I suggested them to the family saying, "This is a great one... you'll love it." Every time I said that, one of my kids would pipe up and say, "That movie is dumb." They were saying this simply because they hadn't chosen it. They had never seen the movie, and knew nothing about it. The crazy thing is that then the younger kids got it stuck in their heads that they wouldn't like the movie either and joined their older sibling in opposing the movie choice. Their thinking dictated their behavior as they all formed strong negative perceptions about the movie without any true knowledge of it.

In the same way, the way we think about ourselves dictates our behavior.

If you believe you are lazy, you will probably act lazy.

If you believe you are the class clown, you will probably fool around all the time.

If you believe you are a leader, you will probably insert yourself in leadership opportunities.

If you believe you are messy, you will probably live a messy, unorganized life.

If you believe you are smart, you will probably study harder and work smarter.

If you believe you are worthless, you will probably not take care of yourself.

And if you believe you are joyful, you'll probably carry joy with you throughout your day.

This is not just about mind over matter, this is a Biblical principle that your thinking and your beliefs precede and predict your behaviors.

This week we're going to consider five principles of the inner image and we're going to observe these principles in the life of King David from the Old Testament. The place where we pick up this story is way before David is King. David is not King David as we know him in much of the Old Testament, he's just David. He's the youngest of eight brothers, a shepherd, and no one of great significance when he arrives on the scene.

Let me set the stage for you. The nation of Israel is in a national crisis as they are on the brink of war with the Philistines. They are currently at a literal standstill. The Israelites stand atop one hillside and the Philistines on the opposite hillside. Each day, a Philistine warrior by the name of Goliath (who was a real nine-foot giant) would come down into the valley between the two nations and shout blasphemies against the God of

Israel. His taunts would end each day with an invitation to send a warrior down into the valley for a one-on-one battle to the death for the win. Whichever warrior won this one-on-one combat, their nation would rule over the other.

David's father Jesse gives David a really important mission: bring lunch to your brothers on the front line. That's right, David is the delivery man. David arrives just in time for Goliath's daily taunt and when he hears it, he is outraged. Now, he's the youngest, the smallest, and the least important in his family, but his inner image outshines all the others. His view of himself and his identity is a whole lot bigger than he is.

Way before David ever faces the giant, he already sees himself as a giant slayer. This is because of what he has experienced in his life... check it out in 1 Samuel 17:34-37:

34 "But David said to Saul, 'Your servant has been keeping his father's sheep. When a lion or a bear came and carried off a sheep from the flock, 35 I went after it, struck it and rescued the sheep from its mouth. When it turned on me, I seized it by its hair, struck it and killed it. 36 Your servant has killed both the lion and the bear; this uncircumcised Philistine will be like one of them, because he has defied the armies of the living God. 37 The LORD who rescued me from the paw of the lion and the paw of the bear will rescue me from the hand of this Philistine.'
Saul said to David, 'Go, and the LORD be with you.'"

Notice what David does: he attributes God's faithfulness to providing the victory over the lion and the bear and carries it right into his current situation.

God hasn't changed, although the scenery has.

The first principle of the inner image is this:
Principle #1: Winning private battles precedes winning public battles.

Long before David faced Goliath, David faced the lion and the bear. And long before David became known in public as the giant slayer, he was slaying giants in private.

It's what you do in private that sets up your inner image for a public victory. The truth is, no one will see the time you've put into building the foundation of a healthy inner self. But the more time you "put in" where no one will see, the more you are set up for a good "output" where everyone will see.

Consider Michael Phelps. He's the most decorated Olympic swimmer of all time. But before he became a highly decorated Olympian, he was just an athlete training alone in a pool. In fact, he trained six hours a day in the pool, six days a week, without fail. During his intense workout routines he would burn 12,000 calories. Talk about putting in the time where no one would see it, to prepare for a victory that everyone would see on the Olympic stage.

Where you win in private, you will win in public.

Spiritually speaking, this means when we think about ourselves and our situation through the same lens that God sees us, and we do this in private, we actually set ourselves up for a future and potentially public victory.

When I think about myself as loved, forgiven, one who has been offered grace and filled with grace, I start to behave in a loving way, willing to offer forgiveness, and gracious to those around me. But that takes some mental training to think rightly about yourself when no one is looking, so you will respond rightly when everyone is looking.

If what you think about yourself is unbecoming, you should probably think about trading in your thoughts for some new ones. You might want to trade in your perspective and pick up God's perspective.

DAILY DISCOVERY: Write down a few beliefs you have about yourself. Are those inner and private beliefs setting you up for public victory or public failure? Let's take a big step of faith today and believe that God has a great and good plan for your life. Today ask God to instill two or three new thought patterns, beliefs about yourself, and perspectives He has of you. Now remind yourself of those beliefs all throughout the day. Those private wins will set you up for a public win.

SKEPTIC'S CHALLENGE/ PRAYER: *"God, if you are real, show me one or two beliefs I've had about myself that are destructive, that are a result of the enemy wanting to steal, kill, or destroy Your plans for my life. What is one thing (or belief) I can change in private that will set me up for a win in public?"*

NOTES

WEEK FIVE / DAY TWO

THE INNER IMAGE:
TAKE OFF FOR OUR SAKE WHAT WE PUT
ON FOR ANOTHER

"David fastened on his sword over the tunic and tried walking around, because he was not used to them.

'I cannot go in these,' he said to Saul, 'because I am not used to them.' So he took them off."

1 SAMUEL 17:39

It was the first semester of middle school and my world seemed to change overnight. In elementary school, it seemed like every kid was your good friend. We had all grown up together and we had been together forever. Then we started middle school, and a whole slew of elementary school kids from many different schools were thrown together into a new massive school setting. All the previous relationships, statuses, and perspectives seemed to go out the window. All these formerly kind and good kids seemed to learn to swear overnight. It became a dog-eat-dog world in moments, as kids who had forever been friends turned on one another and started treating each other in whatever way necessary to quickly establish popularity, a secure friend group, or a dominant position among their peers.

I was taken aback, but I was also not a fool and unwilling to be eaten for lunch by the other kids, so I became a quick learner. I learned how to tear someone down (but not too far down, I wasn't a complete jerk) to build myself up. I learned how to walk the walk and talk the talk and worked my way into the upper echelon of the sixth grade class. Now, I wasn't in the popular group, but I was close enough not to be destroyed day in and day out at school.

But I had a problem. The problem was: that persona was not really me.

Sure, I had added some words to my vocabulary, made a few important wardrobe purchases, figured out the right "strut" for walking down the halls, and knew who I could now talk to and who I shouldn't talk to, but at the end of the day, it just wasn't me.

Have you ever behaved in a way that was totally not you for someone else's sake?

The second principle of the inner image is crucial, it is:

Principle #2: We must take off for our sake that which has been put on for someone else's sake.

Remember David from yesterday and the battle that he is getting ready to face with Goliath? In that day and age if you are going into one-on-one combat to the death, you had better be prepared or at least look the part to instill some confidence in your men. That's exactly what King Saul tries to do with David. We pick the story up in 1 Samuel 17:38-39:

38"Then Saul dressed David in his own tunic. He put a coat of armor on him and a bronze helmet on his head. 39 David fastened on his sword over the tunic and tried walking around, because he was not used to them.
'I cannot go in these,' he said to Saul, 'because I am not used to them.' So he took them off."

What Saul is doing is trying to make David look like a warrior. He is trying to get David to wear his own armor. But David replies by saying, "I can't go out in these." A.k.a., this is not me. David knew that God didn't give him his first victories pretending to be something that he was not. God gave David success being himself… being a shepherd.

If we want our inner image (the way we view ourselves) to be healthy, we need to get rid of everything we've added to our actions and behaviors that isn't us. We need to get rid of everything that we are faking, or at least address everything that we've added to our lives that we did for someone else, to please someone else, or to fit in with someone else.

The things I'm really referring to are the bad behaviors or thoughts about yourself that are really not you nor who God has made you to be.

For teens, it might be acting disrespectfully to teachers or parents because that's what their peers all do. For siblings, it may be fighting with one another because that's how culture says siblings are supposed to treat each other. For guys, it might be acting super macho, crude in language, or chauvinistic because that's what culture tells them to do. For ladies, it might be gossiping with other ladies just to fit in. The point is, most of us have added something to the image we portray about ourselves that is not who God intended us to be. It's time we take off for our own sake the things we added for someone else's sake.

DAILY DISCOVERY: What behaviors or beliefs do you carry that you don't think honors God? Let's believe big that God wants to free us of bad thought patterns or behaviors that we've added to our lives that actually rob us of who we were designed to be. Ask God to show you today what cultural behaviors need to be taken off and what your true God-designed identity might be.

SKEPTIC'S CHALLENGE/ PRAYER: *"God, if You designed me perfectly, would You show me where my image of myself has become corrupted? How do I behave that was never a part of your plan for me? Would You show me something I've put on for someone else that I need to take off?"*

NOTES

WEEK FIVE / DAY THREE

THE INNER IMAGE:
CARRY WHAT GOD USED IN YOUR PAST INTO
YOUR FUTURE

"Then he took his staff in his hand, chose five smooth stones from the
stream, put them in the pouch of his shepherd's bag and, with his sling
in his hand, approached the Philistine."

1 SAMUEL 17:40

One of the things people have said they appreciate about me over the
years is how I communicate in a very real, raw, and authentic way.
It's not uncommon for me to tear up a bit in front of an audience when
I get emotional, laugh at myself when I mix up my words, or share my
own personal fears, struggles, or hurdles with our congregation. It's just
me being me. But with that often comes some clearly imperfect moments
within our church services. Moments that are obviously not planned and
just happen. They are not always the prettiest moments, but they are real
moments.

As our church has grown, so has our planning, strategizing, preparing,
and quality of excellence. With high quality staff and volunteers we
pull off some amazing things. But with that high quality and value for
excellence, we can actually lose some of what makes us "us." We can lose
touch of the things that people have loved most and those are the real,
raw, and imperfect moments that are clearly not planned.

Because our "real, raw, and authentic" moments are what God has
used time and time again in people's lives, it would be foolish of us to
eliminate them in an effort to maintain constant excellence.

There are gifts and abilities that I believe God has uniquely given to each
individual. As a result you've probably seen these God-given gifts used

periodically throughout your life. They could be gifts like mercy, justice, compassion, or leadership.

For me, one of those gifts is the ability to communicate authentically. But my authenticity means I don't usually communicate with polished perfection. This leads to the third principle of the inner image. And it's the reason I still value authenticity in my communication over perfection.

Principle #3: Don't forget to carry the elements God used in your past success into your future battles.

Let's jump back into the story with David as he is preparing to face Goliath.

"Then he took his staff in his hand, chose five smooth stones from the stream, put them in the pouch of his shepherd's bag and, with his sling in his hand, approached the Philistine." 1 SAMUEL 17:40

Notice what David does, he goes right back to the very things God has used in the past that brought him success. In this case it is the weapons of a shepherd. A shepherd would have a sling (basically an old-fashioned slingshot) and a shepherd bag to carry some good stones. A shepherd used a sling to protect his flock and chase away wild animals. This is exactly how David is going to face Goliath, as a shepherd. He's not going to pretend to be anything other than what he is and take along what God has used in his past.

There is something about embracing where you've seen God uniquely work through you in the past that will set you up for a victory in your future.

DAILY DISCOVERY: Consider when and where comments were made about you in a positive light. What were the circumstances? What did you bring that was unique to the situation? What have people said you do really well? When have people thanked you, praised you, or applauded you? Let's believe big that God has given you unique gifts that He loves to see you use in battle. Make sure those God-given gifts are being carried into your next battle.

SKEPTIC'S CHALLENGE/ PRAYER: *"God, if you have uniquely gifted me, remind me where people have pointed out these strengths. Help me not to be afraid to live more in these strengths."*

NOTES

WEEK FIVE / DAY FOUR

THE INNER IMAGE:
BUILD CONFIDENCE IN GOD'S ABILITIES,
NOT YOURS

"David said to the Philistine, 'You come against me with sword and spear and javelin, but I come against you in the name of the LORD Almighty, the God of the armies of Israel, whom you have defied.'"

1 SAMUEL 17:45

Our family is not a huge sports family. We love water sports and outdoor winter activities, but not necessarily formalized team sports. But periodically, we'll play a pick-up game of basketball in the front driveway. When my kids were younger I was of course the one everyone wanted on their team. Not because of my great basketball skills, but because of my height. I was just bigger, stronger, faster, and taller than all of them. It really didn't matter how outnumbered I was, it could be me and the youngest kid against all the others and my team would likely win. That lucky child knew it had little to do with them and had everything to do with whose team they were on. It had everything to do with the fact that they were teamed up with Daddy.

Similarly the fourth principle of the inner image has little to do with what you can do and has everything to do with what your Heavenly Father can do.

The fourth principle is:

Principle #4: Build your confidence in God's abilities, not your abilities.

Back to our story with David facing Goliath. We pick up the story in their first exchange of words.

"David said to the Philistine, 'You come against me with sword and spear and javelin, but I come against you in the name of the LORD Almighty, the God of the armies of Israel, whom you have defied.'" 1 SAMUEL 17:45

David calls out two things here. He calls out where he knows Goliath is getting his confidence and he calls out where he is building his own personal confidence. He says, your (Goliath's) confidence is in your sword, spear and javelin. Now to be fair, Goliath has a massive sword, spear and javelin. The surrounding verses tell us that just the iron tip of Goliath's spear weighed 15 pounds. And the spear itself was like a weaver's rod. That is one heck of a spear. You've got to be really strong to even handle a spear of that weight.

David knows Goliath has his confidence in his size and his weapons. So where is this tiny little shepherd going to find confidence to match Goliath? David goes on to say, "I come against you in the name of the LORD Almighty." David is going to build his confidence on something different. We, like Goliath, have a tendency to build our confidence in what we see, while David chooses to build his confidence in what is unseen.

Our best inner image (or self-perceived identity) is not built on what we see or what we can do, but on God's unseen reality and what He can do.

Do you ever build your confidence in what you can do? You try to solve a business deal with your best strategy, or try to get the promotion with your best career moves, or fix a relationship with your best relational strategies. In doing so we rely on what we see and try to manage it in our own way.

However, if God is who He says He is, if He is all powerful, if He is all knowing, if He is good to us, then when we build our confidence on what we can see or accomplish versus what He sees or could accomplish, we are actually aiming too low.

David didn't aim low at all. He didn't aim to create a way for peace talks to begin, or aim for maybe one decent hit on Goliath. No, he talked some serious smack built not on his abilities, but on God's.

DAILY DISCOVERY: Do you try to manage your own battles with your own abilities? Consider what hurdles you're facing today. Let's take our faith to the extreme and imagine what it would look like to fully trust God not to just make a small breakthrough here, but instead to completely bring a victory to the giant that stands before you. Let's believe in His abilities and not in ours.

SKEPTIC'S CHALLENGE/ PRAYER: *"I always approach things through the lens of what I see and what I can do. God, would you just give me a thought about my struggles, how You see them, and what You can do to overcome them?"*

NOTES

WEEK FIVE / DAY FIVE

THE INNER IMAGE:
HUMBLE YOURSELF TO BE EXALTED

"Whoever exalts himself will be humbled, and whoever humbles himself
will be exalted."

MATTHEW 23:12 (ESV)

If you ever saw the movie "Billy Madison" with Adam Sandler, you
probably remember a peripheral group of characters whose movie
line became synonymous with the movie. That line was "O'Doyle
rules!" O'Doyle was the family of bullies who made life miserable for
younger kids in the school. After each and every bullish action the family
member would throw their hands in the air over their head like they had
just won a boxing match and yell, "O'Doyle rules!"

Near the end of the comedy, the O'Doyle family loses control of their car
when they run over a small banana peel, and plummet off a cliff while
still chanting "O'Doyle rules!" Of course the movie was made in the era
of slap-stick humor. But the idea of this prideful, bullying family getting
what they deserve seems somewhat satisfying.

In the account of David and Goliath, seeing the prideful and bullying
Goliath meet his doom and the underdog David as victorious is also
very satisfying. Now the real question is, how will David respond to this
victory? Is David going to throw his hands in the air and yell "David
Rules?" Is David going to take all the glory and become full of himself?
Check out his response in 1 Samuel 17:46-47.

46 "'This day the LORD will deliver you into my hands, and I'll strike you
down and cut off your head. This very day I will give the carcasses of the
Philistine army to the birds and the wild animals, and the whole world will
know that there is a God in Israel. 47 All those gathered here will know that

it is not by sword or spear that the LORD saves; for the battle is the LORD's, and he will give all of you into our hands.'" 1 SAMUEL 17:46-47

Yes he starts by saying, "here's what I'm going to do to you [strike you down and cut off your head]." But then he goes right on to say, "and the whole world will know that there is a God in Israel... they will know that it is not by sword or spear that the Lord saves; for the battle is the Lord's."

Notice he doesn't say, "everyone will know that I am the best," or instead of "O'Doyle rules!" people will chant, "David rules!" No, he says everyone will know the battle is the Lord's. Everyone will know the work of God.

The fifth principle of the inner image is this:
Principle #5: Whoever humbles himself will be exalted.

If you want to have a good start for your inner image—your true identity—the best foundation is built upon a humble heart and a humble start.

In the Bible we see it this way. Those who consistently redirect glory to God have an abundant supply of glory directed to them. That is true of David. People will be singing his praises and directing glory to him. But one of the things he will consistently do is redirect all that honor and glory back to God. He recognizes that it is God who supplies supernatural victories and that a godly inner image can never be a glory hog.

Perhaps David understands it all so clearly even in the rival he faced. Goliath was a prideful bully. And "Whoever exalts himself will be humbled, and whoever humbles himself will be exalted." Maintaining a humble foundation for your God-given identity is crucial for the long haul of God-given victories and success that He desires to give you.

DAILY DISCOVERY: Where have you been successful in the past? Were you a glory hog in those circumstances? Let's take our faith to the next level and trust that God has amazing plans for you and that these plans include some great God-sized victories. But let's make our commitment right now before God that any and all God-sized victories will result in directing glory and honor to Him and not hogging it for ourselves.

SKEPTIC'S CHALLENGE/ PRAYER: *"God, I've known some people who were filled with pride and full of themselves. They weren't the best to be around. Could you show me the danger of that, any place where it has crept into my life, and help me to start with a foundation of humility in my identity?"*

WEEK FIVE / DAY SIX & SEVEN

DAY 6: LET THAT THOUGHT SIMMER

What idea was most challenging to you this week?

DAY 7: LET THAT THOUGHT SIMMER

What day from this week or concept do you want to rethink about?

WEEK SIX

WEEK SIX / DAY ONE

ROYALTY:
ROYALTY HONORS PURPOSEFULLY

"But you are a chosen people, a royal priesthood, a holy nation, God's special possession, that you may declare the praises of him who called you out of darkness into his wonderful light."

1 PETER 2:9

16 "The Spirit himself bears witness with our spirit that we are children of God, 17 and if children, then heirs—heirs of God and fellow heirs with Christ..."

ROMANS 8:16-17 (ESV)

Last week we spent our time focused on building a solid foundation for our inner image or our identity. The reason this is so important, and the main point of last week, is because you can never grow past your inner image.

This week we are going to be focusing on the principles of royalty as a child of the King of Kings and the Lord of Lords and a representative of His Kingdom.

In 1 Peter 2:9, scripture calls us a royal priesthood. Most of us struggle to think of ourselves as royalty. Royalty seems so distant, ambiguous, and almost medieval. Perhaps it feels even more intangible for those of us in the United States since we are a nation that has never known royalty. It's not a regular part of our vocabulary. Yet if we struggle to wrap our minds around the royalty we carry, we will fail to live in the fullness of that identity.

The contrasting view of royalty would be comparing the mindset of a prince (or princess) to that of a pauper.

Unfortunately many Christians struggle between these perspectives. I believe we either carry a prince (or princess) mentality or a pauper mentality.

Here's some ways they are different:

A prince or princess is a son or daughter of significance.

A pauper is a son or daughter of insignificance.

A prince or princess owns everything the king owns and functions from a place of ownership.

A pauper has little and functions from a place of lack (a mindset that things will always run out).

A prince or princess can speak on behalf of their father.

A pauper lacks a voice.

A prince or princess carries themselves with confidence and healthy pride of the family they represent.

A pauper is timid, shy, embarrassed by their family and insecure in their identity.

If you're a royal priesthood (royal people) there is a mindset as a prince or princess that goes with your royalty.

This week we'll consider 5 Principles of Royalty.

The first principle is this:

Principle #1: Royalty Honors Purposefully

"Honor everyone. Love the brotherhood. Fear God. Honor the emperor."
1 PETER 2:17 (ESV)

This verse is found right in the context of the declaration that "you are a chosen people, a royal priesthood."

Peter, who is writing this letter, gives some examples in the context of what it looks like to honor everyone.

In verses 13-14 he says, "Be subject for the LORD's sake to every human institution, whether it be to the emperor as supreme, 14 or to governors…" (ESV)

In verse 18 he says, "Servants, be subject to your masters with all respect, not only to the good and gentle but also to the unjust." (ESV)

You might think 2020 and 2021 were difficult years to live lives honoring others as those years were filled with such malice, hatred, and anger. However, we have it pretty good in comparison to Peter's day.

In Peter's day, the government was oppressive and domineering, led by dictators who were pride-filled, power-hungry men. Work life was not a whole lot better, as most employers carried the same attitude and demeanor as cruel governing leaders. Slavery was still commonplace and the positions of servants and masters were normal.

It's into these relationships that often lacked honor, Peter calls us up to a royal lifestyle to honor purposefully.

The most important sentence in these verses is a short two-word sentence buried in verse 17. "Fear God."

The Greek word for *fear* doesn't necessarily have to be translated "be afraid," it can be translated as "stand in awe of or reverence for." It's this idea that I have great reverence for my God, and since I have great reverence for Him, the creator of humanity, I must honor His creation, no matter their position.

As royalty we don't give honor based on who they are, we give honor based on who their creator is.

A royal mindset believes: royalty honors, recognizing that to whatever you honor, you ascribe worth.

Christ's sacrifice on the cross for humanity tells of the worth of each individual. A royal identity recognizes that to ascribe honor, is to ascribe God's view of worth over humanity.

As royalty, part of our responsibility is helping people see their own worth. When we honor them we ascribe worth to them.

Question: Who in your life would be taken off guard if you paid honor to them? Who have you withheld honor from, but now (as royalty) need to honor purposefully?

One of the crazy ways we best represent our Father's kingdom is to honor those who by worldly standards don't deserve an ounce of honor, but by heavenly standards, honor should be given.

Consider the following people or positions you and I are called to honor: the president, teachers, a bad boss, parents, siblings, disrespectful coworkers or peers, those rotten kids in school, someone in business who wronged you, and the list could go on and on. You get the idea: we are people who show honor because that's part of our royal responsibility.

DAILY DISCOVERY: Today I want to challenge you to step into a new identity, perhaps an identity you've never worn before, and that is as royalty. If you were a prince or princess of an actual nation, how would your mindset change overnight? Now carry that royal mindset by focusing on honoring purposefully, understanding that those who you honor you ascribe worth to. See how many people you can show honor to in a unique and special way today.

SKEPTIC'S PRAYER/ CHALLENGE: There are many people who don't deserve your honor. However, try putting on an identity that is of a much higher calling and purpose. Try showing honor to a few people today who are not deserving one way or another of your honor. How did it make you feel to step into a different mindset of honor? Did you do it on your own or did you sense God in the midst of it?

WEEK SIX / DAY TWO

ROYALTY:
ROYALTY EXECUTES EAGERLY

"I will give you the keys of the kingdom of heaven; whatever you bind on earth will be bound in heaven, and whatever you loose on earth will be loosed in heaven."

MATTHEW 16:19

One of the things that drives me nuts as a parent is when my kids litter in our own home. I'm not just talking about kids leaving their toys out, it's when they open a piece of candy and throw the wrapper right on the floor. I understand that when you're eating lots of individually wrapped pieces of candy, you're not going to walk to the trash in between each piece to throw away the individual wrapper. But for crying out loud, they could collect all the wrappers on the side tables sitting right beside them and when finished, take the collected wrappers to the trash. But NOOOOO, they just peel that candy open and throw the wrapper near their feet like they don't care at all.

I'll speak up and say, "Guys, don't just throw your wrappers on the floor, this is your house too." Because that's the point, right? Yes, my name might be on the deed to the home, but as my children, it is their house too. As residents of the home, my hope would be that they carry a sense of ownership of the home and responsibility for it.

In the same way, God may be the ruler over His Kingdom, but as residents of His Kingdom and as royal members of His family, He too is calling us to take ownership and responsibility for the Kingdom.

The second principle of royalty is:

Principle #2: Royalty Executes Eagerly

God is looking for His children to make decisions as He would. He is looking for His children to fix problems as He would. He wants His children to love, forgive, honor, bring hope, heal, and restore on His behalf.

In the book of Mark, Jesus is teaching and crowds have gathered to listen. And it's no small crowd. More than 5,000 people are hanging on Jesus' every word. In that day and age it's not like 5,000 people can just run to town in between Jesus' messages and go through the drive through for a quick bite to eat. Feeding 5,000 people is no small task today, and would have been an even bigger task back then. But Jesus goes to his disciples and drops a bomb of a statement on them. He says to them in Mark 6:37, "You give them something to eat." Overwhelmed by the request, they respond by saying, "It would take six months of wages to feed this crowd."

Understanding where this takes place in the timeline of their time with Jesus is important. By this point they have seen Jesus perform miracles regularly. In fact, just the month before, Jesus sent out the disciples themselves to perform miracles and proclaim the Kingdom of heaven is near. By their own hands they saw many miraculous things. But now they are faced with a monumental hurdle of feeding a crowd and they do nothing.

Something to keep in mind every time we read the Bible is every time Jesus asked a question or posed an opportunity it was not because he didn't know the answer, it was always because there was a very real and tangible answer and solution to the situation. So in this case, when Jesus tells the disciples to feed the crowds, He's not saying it to cause them to fail, He's saying it because it is the very thing that is within reach for them to achieve a victory.

He's looking for them to execute on behalf of His Kingdom what is within reach. The best approach for royalty is to always try to execute Kingdom realities on behalf of the King.

The royal mindset is that royalty unashamedly takes the bold first step in executing kingdom realities. Royalty doesn't have to wait for permission for the King to execute His heart over a matter.

Perhaps you remember the story of "The Prince and The Pauper." The story features two boys who look exactly alike. One grows up as the prince in the kingdom and the other on the streets as a pauper. One day they run into each other and decide to switch places. When the prince, now living as a pauper, is out in the kingdom and sees the needs of his people, his mindset is simply to execute a kingdom solution on the spot. Of course he has no power and is heartbroken that he can't do anything to help meet the needs.

We are not without power to help meet the needs in our world. We are royalty and representatives of God's Kingdom. If you carry a pauper's mindset you probably assume there is nothing you can do to help fix the broken things in our world. Perhaps you just sit on the sidelines of life waiting upon the Lord, waiting for the King to show up and do something. But one of the things the King did was send you and me to fix the brokenness that permeates our world.

What could that look like? For me it is often simply asking God, "What does this situation look like in heaven?" And then I ask Him to align my reality with His reality. I ask Him to bring His heavenly Kingdom to this earthly kingdom. Jesus even taught us to pray that way. Pray, "Your kingdom come, your will be done, on earth as it is in heaven." MATTHEW 6:10

Many times I don't know what God's exact solution is for a situation. In those cases I simply pray for Him to work in ways I've seen in scripture. Or I pray for Him to demonstrate His power in line with His character. All of these prayers are simply an effort to execute a solution for His kingdom as a royal prince or princess would.

DAILY DISCOVERY: What is one small thing that is broken or needs a solution in your life? If Jesus were standing beside you, what type of solution do you think He might bring to it? Now take a few big steps of faith today to try to execute His Kingdom wherever you go, knowing you are royalty.

SKEPTIC'S CHALLENGE/ PRAYER: Is it possible God has a heavenly solution for every earthly problem we face? Is there something that has perplexed you for quite some time? Would you consider taking a leap of faith by asking God to give you even a small insight into a solution for the problem you are facing?

NOTES

WEEK SIX / DAY THREE

ROYALTY:
ROYALTY CARRIES CONFIDENTLY

4 "Such confidence we have through Christ before God. 5 Not that we are competent in ourselves to claim anything for ourselves, but our competence comes from God. 6 He has made us competent as ministers of a new covenant…"

2 CORINTHIANS 3:4-6

Some people are just innately self-confident in life. I've seen it in my kids at different times. One child will walk right up to anyone and start up a conversation and others will hide behind me, barely peeking out around me when meeting someone for the first time.

No matter where you land on a scale of natural confidence, as royalty you are about to get an upgrade in the realm of kingdom confidence.

Principle #3: Royalty Carries Confidently

The apostle Paul, when writing to the church in Corinth, says, "Our competence comes from God."

Here's the Kingdom principle: Kingdom confidence is found in Kingdom competence, and your competence comes from God.

I think there are tons of Christians who feel incompetent. Maybe you feel like, "I don't know enough, I'm not spiritual enough, I wish I understood more about the Bible." The Apostle Paul says, "Our competence comes from God."

In fact, this is regularly the common denominator in scripture. God uses people that don't know enough, aren't educated enough, aren't qualified enough (they feel incompetent), etc.

And it's an observation made about Peter and John in Acts 4.

"When they saw the courage of Peter and John and realized that they were unschooled, ordinary men, they were astonished and they took note that these men had been with Jesus." ACTS 4:13

Do you see it? They were unschooled, ordinary men. To the crowds, their astonishment comes from the fact that these guys didn't carry the competence to do what they were doing and preach the way they were preaching. Yet it is Kingdom competence that causes Kingdom confidence.

The first time you do anything you usually feel pretty incompetent. But time and experience builds competence, and as a result, builds confidence.

I remember the first funeral I did as a pastor. Even though I had a degree from a Bible college and knew quite a bit about scripture, I had no idea how to minister to a family in a time of loss. I had no idea what elements were a part of a funeral message or memorial service. I kept thinking, "Good thing the person already died, so they don't have to witness my incompetent display of pastoring at their funeral."

It probably wasn't as bad as I felt it was. In fact, the Lord gave me a grace and a competence for that moment. And His competence has given me confidence for more of those moments. Kingdom confidence cannot come according to what you can do, but according to what He can do through you.

The royal mindset is this: royalty develops confidence as we release our own view of ourselves and our abilities and pick up His view of ourselves with His abilities.

DAILY DISCOVERY: Here's where taking your faith to the extreme might feel crazy. I want to challenge you to live today like you are the most confident person on the planet. You have a confidence not of your own, nor based on your own competence but on who God is and who He says you are. You are royalty, and royalty carries themselves confidently.

SKEPTIC'S CHALLENGE/ PRAYER: Where do you feel insecure in life? Where do you lack self-confidence? Would you consider asking God to give you a sense of security or confidence in that area today? If you feel more confident in that area, is it possible God is really providing a competence from His world to give you a confidence in your world?

NOTES

WEEK SIX / DAY FOUR

ROYALTY:
ROYALTY LIVES ABUNDANTLY

"And God is able to bless you abundantly, so that in all things at all times, having all that you need, you will abound in every good work."

2 CORINTHIANS 9:8

"...I came that they may have life and have it abundantly."

JOHN 10:10b (ESV)

Have you ever asked someone, "How are you doing?" and they reply with "We're getting by," "We're making it," or "We'll pull through." Now I agree with those statements if you're talking about an attitude of endurance while facing hardships in life. However, I disagree with you if you're talking about the quality of personal wellness (in mind and heart) as you endure through the hardship.

Our culture lives in a constant state of longing for more. This is a perspective of lack. It's a pauper's mindset. In fact, companies market toward a pauper mindset, telling you that their product will bring the satisfaction, security, or happiness that you've been looking for. But God's Kingdom is one of abundance where you as royalty lack nothing.

Some might say, Jesus lived a poor lifestyle where he really had nothing. But, did Jesus model what it looked like to live with nothing, or did he model what it looked like for Him to do what God called Him to, knowing He had access to everything? While all of Jesus' ministry years were on the road without many earthly possessions, I believe He lived knowing He belonged to a Kingdom of great abundance.

Just like when He was faced with a hungry crowd of over 5,000 people and His disciples told him it would take six months' wages to feed them, His Kingdom provides for the need. I think any one of us would be incredibly grateful if six months' worth of your wages showed up in your bank account later today. I believe Jesus lived knowing he could access six months' worth of wages any day of the week. He understood the kingdom of abundance that He belonged to.

Principle #4: Royalty Lives Abundantly

In John 10:10, Jesus says that he has come that we might have life and have it abundantly. When Jesus is talking about abundance, it is more than just material wealth. It's much more holistic than that.

I need God to provide me with an abundance of grace for an obnoxious person.

I need God to provide me with an abundance of patience for my kids.

I need God to provide me with an abundance of resources for my needs today.

I need God to provide me with an abundance of wisdom I need for my decisions.

I need God to provide me with an abundance of forgiveness to offer to the person who wronged me.

I need the abundance of His Kingdom in all things, its fullness and satisfaction of mind, body, and soul.

It's everything you need to thrive in your thinking.

It's everything you need to thrive in your relationships.

It's everything you need to thrive in your daily needs.

It's everything you need to thrive in everything!

I find I have to remind myself regularly that my heavenly Father has an abundance of wisdom for what I'm facing, He has an abundance of financial resources for what I'm facing, He has an abundance of grace, patience, love, forgiveness, and endurance all at my fingertips.

The Kingdom mindset is: When your eyes are fixed on what you might lose (perspective of lack) you'll never see all that you have (perspective of abundance).

You will only try to bring the Kingdom in whatever measure you believe you have access to it and to what measure you believe the Kingdom contains. If you think you have access to little, you'll ask for little, and if you think you have access to much, you will ask and expect for much.

If you think sparingly and pray sparing prayers, it will be manifest around you sparingly. However, if you pray abundantly, you will likely start to experience the Kingdom of abundance that you belong to.

It is time to release the pauper mindset of lack and scarcity and put on the mindset of royalty. You belong to the Kingdom of abundance.

DAILY DISCOVERY: Where do you lack in your life today? Do you lack material needs, emotional needs, relational needs? Let's take a big step of faith today and believe that there is Kingdom abundance available to help meet every one of those needs. As royalty, it is yours. Ask for it. Pray great big prayers that reach into a Kingdom of great abundance.

SKEPTIC'S CHALLENGE/ PRAYER: Where do you lack in your life today? Do you carry a pauper mindset of lack? Do you fall to marketers who play off of the pauper mindset? If you lack something in your life today, is it possible God could provide abundantly for you? Perhaps now is the time to ask Him to, or ask Him to show you how His Kingdom can provide abundance of love, grace, forgiveness, patience, and so much more.

WEEK SIX / DAY FIVE

ROYALTY:
ROYALTY ARE PEOPLE OF PEACE

"Blessed are the peacemakers,
for they shall be called children of God."
MATTHEW 5:9

"For the kingdom of God is not a matter of eating and drinking, but of righteousness, peace and joy in the Holy Spirit."
ROMANS 14:17

I'm an eight on the enneagram assessment. Eights are challengers. It doesn't take a rocket scientist to know what that means, it means I like to challenge things and challenge people. In my family, I'm not the only one. You can just imagine what happens when a couple of eights get in a room together. We can start talking about what color we should paint the walls, but before you know it we are not just talking about our color preferences, we are arguing about the colors. We are forming deep convictions and beliefs around our preferences for the wall color. We are arguing over the nuances of why one shade is far superior to another shade. We are debating flat, shell, glossy, and satin finishes. We are debating brands and application methods. We are talking about whether we should use painter's tape or just edge it by hand.

Some of you had no idea there were so many elements we could fight about and disagree over. Well there are, because I'm an eight. Unfortunately my eight personality sometimes pushes against this final principle of royalty.

Principle #5: Royalty are People of Peace

Jesus says at the beginning of the most famous sermon he ever preached, the Sermon on the Mount, "Blessed are the peacemakers, for they will be called children of God." Something that makes children of God and representatives of His Kingdom distinct is their ability to bring peace. We promote it, we procure it, we are people who carry it. We are people of peace.

In Romans 14, the followers of Christ are in a disagreement. No, it's not over a paint color. It's over whether or not you could eat certain kinds of meat. Jews had lived their entire lives up until this point eating Kosher diets, meaning there were some foods Jews didn't eat. After the death and resurrection of Christ, God lifted those restrictions that previously had set apart the nation of Israel. As God wants to extend his grace and mercy to all of mankind, He removes all dietary restrictions that might become stumbling blocks to Gentiles coming to Christ. However, some Jews were pretty set in their ways and continued to call certain foods (like bacon) unclean. On a side note, I'm so grateful bacon is no longer considered an unclean food (all the bacon lovers just shouted AMEN!). To put an end to this argument, the Apostle Paul says, it's not about the type of foods that you have or don't have, but let me tell you about things you must have. You must have PEACE. For the Kingdom of God is about righteousness, peace, and joy.

There are plenty of things we can argue about in culture. But one thing that should stand out in our behavior as children of God is not how we argue, but how we bring peace.

When you think about royalty, being a person who carries peace is critical. One of the primary duties for presidents, royalty, or national rulers is to make sure to uphold peace between nations or at the very least work toward that end. Maybe I've watched too many movies, but I can easily imagine a royal delegation who goes to meet with the royalty from a neighboring nation. In their discussion they are using wisdom, grace, and diplomacy to work together and maintain peace.

As royalty and representatives of God's Kingdom it is our calling to be people of peace.

Does it mean you'll never disagree with anyone? No, that's not the point. Jesus disagreed with people all the time, but He always delivered His first challenge to them on a platter of peace. He was always trying to introduce them to the Kingdom and His first introduction always carried His peace.

My wife has said of me that I can bring resolution and peace to almost any relational conflict. That no matter how mad people are when they start a conversation with me, I can usually lead the conversation in a direction where everyone feels heard and appreciated, and relationships are usually restored. Of course, I'm not batting 1,000 in that area, no one is. But I do pretty well.

I attribute my success in it to a simple prayer. I pray, "God, help me to be a person of peace to them today. Help me to see things from their perspective. And help me to bring the peace that I represent into this relationship." Perhaps it's a simple prayer like that which actually ushers in God's Kingdom peace to a circumstance that brings restoration or resolution.

If 2020 and 2021 showed us anything, it is that our culture can fight, argue, and war with one another about anything and everything. As royalty, it is time we act like the royal delegation that we are, the kingdom we represent, and be peacemakers.

DAILY DISCOVERY: Who, where, or what needs peace in your life today? Let's believe big that we actually carry something today that could tangibly bring peace there. *God, would you give us the wisdom, grace, and diplomacy to be the peacemakers that we truly are?*

SKEPTIC'S CHALLENGE/ PRAYER: Who, where, or what needs peace in your life today? Is it possible that God may have a path of bringing peace to that person, place, or thing? Try praying, *"God, if You are real, would You show me a first step in bringing peace there?"*

WEEK SIX / DAY SIX & SEVEN

DAY 6: LET THAT THOUGHT SIMMER

What idea was most challenging to you this week?

DAY 7: LET THAT THOUGHT SIMMER

What day from this week or concept do you want to rethink about?

NOTES

WEEK SEVEN

WEEK SEVEN / DAY ONE

FAITH VS. FEAR:
FUELING FAITH OR FEAR

We all understand the concept that fire needs fuel to burn. In the summer, my kids will regularly ask if we can have a bonfire at night. I honestly think it's less to do with the fire itself or being with family and much more to do with eating s'mores. Sometimes my response is driven by whether I want to embrace smelling like a bonfire or whether we have ingredients for s'mores, but more often than not it is driven by whether or not I have wood that will burn well.

My kids haven't quite figured out that the fuel you add to a fire matters. Sometimes my kids will ask about having a bonfire in the evening while it is pouring rain in the middle of the day, to which I respond in complete confusion with, "Nothing will burn, everything is soaked out there!" They don't fully get it that the fuel matters.

In the same way, we can be purposeful with the fuel we add to our lives. The fuel we add will help produce in us faith or fear. You will always operate from the vantage point of either faith or fear. I think it would behoove us to know what has the tendency to fuel one or the other. And what you will likely find is that you are producing and growing an identity around what you are primarily fueling.

In addition to the awareness of the fuel you're throwing on the fire of your heart, there is one other primary element you should be aware of that sets the stage for building an identity of faith or an identity of fear. The setting of the stage for these identity-building moments have often come to be called crucible moments.

Studies have been done and surveys have been taken and revealed that there are specific moments in our lives that have the tendency to grow us in faith or fear. These moments are at the core of building our identities... they are crucible moments.

WHAT ARE CRUCIBLE MOMENTS?

Some of the primary categories that capture what a crucible moment might be are the following:

1. **Tragic Moments.** This could be a bad health diagnosis, a loss of a job, a sudden loss of a loved one, a financial crisis, a child in rebellion, etc.

2. **Celebration Moments.** This could be the birth of a baby, a promotion at work, a financial breakthrough, an anniversary, etc.

3. **Transition/Change Moments.** This could be moving to a new city, getting a new job, moving to a new house, changing schools, a shift in your friendships, etc.

4. **Challenging Moments.** This could be having to sit down for a difficult conversation with a loved one, being charged with more responsibility at work, being asked to coach your child's sports team, leading something for the first time, etc.

All of these can be crucible moments, and they all have the ability to fuel our faith or fear.

For today, let's simply assess the landscape of our lives and start by identifying a crucible moment from your past and how it shaped your identity for the good or the bad.

Follow that up by assessing your present and potential future. This is looking at the landscape ahead. For example, are you starting a new job in a month and along with it, moving to a new home, a new school district for your children, a new everything? While it may seem really exciting, this has all the signs of being a crucible moment in your life and your family. This is a great time to prepare your heart to grow in a healthy way during this upcoming crucible moment.

You're likely going to throw some fuel on the fire of your heart during these crucible moments. Let's be purposeful to throw fuel that will build healthy faith-filled identities vs. fear-filled identities.

DAILY DISCOVERY: Identify a crucible moment from your past. How did it shape your identity for the good or the bad? What fuel was being added to your heart during that season?

If you have a potential crucible moment ahead of you on the horizon of your life, let's take a big step of faith and start throwing the right fuel on our hearts now in preparation for those moments to become healthy, identity-building moments.

SKEPTIC'S CHALLENGE/ PRAYER: This week we're looking at what fuels faith vs. fear. You may not even like the term *faith*. Perhaps you would consider substituting the word *divine* throughout the week. It's simply the idea that God could be a part of the equation. Maybe you've heard the terms divine appointment, divine inspiration, divine intervention, etc. Consider how God might be wanting to do something divine in your life during these crucible moments. Where has your identity been formed for the good or the bad in crucible moments? Do you think the divine was ever using crucible moments to grow something healthy in your identity?

NOTES

WEEK SEVEN / DAY TWO

FAITH VS. FEAR:
THE FUEL OF WHAT YOU MEDITATE ON

"Elijah said, 'As the LORD Almighty lives, whom I serve,...'"
1 KINGS 18:15

This week, as we consider what fuels faith vs. fear, we are going to be diving into the account of the prophet Elijah. Much of his life story is captured in I Kings chapters 17-19. Before we get there, let me ask a question: have you ever had a traumatic experience in the past that impacted a future experience?

Last winter, my daughter (16 years old at the time) joined a friend for an afternoon and evening of downhill skiing. Now, you have to know that up to this point, downhill skiing was not a regular part of our lives. For her, it had been years since she had been skiing. To say she was a "newbie" was an understatement. She did what anyone would do starting out in a sport. She started small on the bunny hills, then worked her way up to the green runs (easiest), and then to the blue (medium). After a few hours of skiing these moderate hills, the day was coming to a close and the group she was with said, "Let's all head down a black diamond." Now, these are Wisconsin hills, so our black diamonds are still really reasonable. The task, while challenging for her, was no doubt within her ability.

Boldly, yet nervously, she went for it. Unfortunately, halfway down the hill, her hat started to fly off due to her speed. In an effort to hold onto her hat, she lost her focus on the hill and the skiing at hand. She barreled down the hill gaining speed, lost control, and ran right into a light pole in the middle of the hill. With a loud crash, skis and poles flew, and her body glanced off the pole. In short, the pole won and left her with a fractured pelvis and hip and broken leg. It was quite a traumatic experience as well as a long and difficult road to recovery.

However, today she is completely recovered. While she may have physically recovered, she still hasn't skied that same run at the ski hill. In fact, this year our family has returned to that ski hill quite a few times and the first time was very significant for my daughter. It wasn't just about getting back onto skis, it was about the entire experience and all it represented to her. She had to face her fears, face her insecurities, and quite literally face that mountain again.

What you think about when you are in the middle of a crucible moment may be the most important thing that influences the type of fuel you are throwing on the fire of your heart.

And your past is often the #1 place where you will find the fuel to use.

Let's dive into the story of Elijah. Elijah is a prophet in the Old Testament. Prophets were the individuals God chose to use as His mouthpiece to speak to the Kings and the nations on His behalf. He would give them messages, challenges, warnings, prophetic information for the future, and promises from God that would all be delivered from the prophet.

In 1 Kings 16:29-34, we are introduced to a king by the name of Ahab. He is the king of Israel, but he is not leading his people to follow the God of the Israelites. Instead he is leading his people to worship Baal and establish other worship practices to worship other false gods. This provoked the LORD, the God of Israel, to anger. So God sent a message through the prophet Elijah to try to get the attention of this wicked king.

The message was simple. There will be no more rain in the land until I (the prophet Elijah) say so. Then, led by the Lord, Elijah goes into hiding, which is a good place to be when you are the only one who can turn the water back on for the nation. There will be a lot of people who are going to be mad and they are going to be looking for someone to blame and someone (Elijah) to fix the problem.

He doesn't go into hiding for just a week, no, Elijah is in hiding for three years. During those years the Lord provided for Elijah in a few miraculous ways. For a season he got his water from a brook and God sent ravens to Elijah as his provision of food. For another season, he stayed with a widow and her son, and God miraculously provided flour and oil that never ran out for them to make bread.

While Elijah is away, Ahab is furious and on the hunt for Elijah. In his anger he is killing other servants of God. Obadiah, who is in charge of Ahab's palace, loves God and actually is doing everything he can do behind the scenes to save anyone's life who is in danger from angry Ahab.

Obadiah and Elijah had very different experiences over these three years that Elijah was in hiding. Obadiah's experience of pain caused fear to rule his heart, while Elijah's experience of provision from God caused great faith to rule his heart.

If I could turn this into a principle for fueling Faith vs. Fear, I would say it this way...

Principle #1: What you meditate on from the past fuels Faith or Fear.

To meditate is to re-think about something. It is to digest that information over and over again.

In this case Elijah is choosing to meditate on God's faithful provision, while Obadiah is meditating on the loss of life he has seen and the constant state of fear he has been in. The reality is meditation on provision from the past fuels faith... and meditation on pain from the past fuels fear.

If I remind myself of places where I've seen God provide in my life in the past, I find faith and confidence starting to rise within me. However, if I remind myself of places of hurt and pain and re-think about the pain it caused, fear will start to creep in and rule my heart.

After my daughter's accident, one of the comments we heard over and over from the doctors was their astonishment that her injuries weren't worse. Her friend actually caught the whole thing on video, and when watching it, you can understand why the doctors say that. If she would have hit that pole a few inches in a different direction, it could have killed her. Instead, she only had a few breaks, no internal bleeding, she was only in a wheelchair for a week, only on crutches for a week after that, only in a walking boot for a week after that… only, only, only. Yes she experienced a lot of pain, but we also saw so much of God's provision in that season. My daughter could have focused all of her attention on the pain of her injury and accident and allowed it to paralyze her from ever moving forward and putting on another pair of skis. She could have meditated all on her pain and allowed fear to rule her heart. Or she could focus on God's provision, even in the midst of the pain, and face that mountain again, with faith ruling her heart.

DAILY DISCOVERY: Think back to a crucible moment from your past. Now, where was God providing for you in the midst of it? If you find yourself once again facing another crucible moment, meditate today (re-think) about God's provision of the past. If you're not in the midst of a crucible moment, still, meditate on God's provision from your past and allow it to stir a bolder faith in you as you face today.

SKEPTIC'S CHALLENGE/ PRAYER: When you think of your past, do you have a tendency to rehearse thoughts of the pain of your past or the good (divine provision) of your past? Today, make a list of provisions you've experienced in your life. Is it possible that it was divine in nature? Now allow that list to renew your heart with confidence for today.

NOTES

WEEK SEVEN / DAY THREE

FAITH VS. FEAR:
THE FUEL OF THE URGENT

"'...How long will you waiver between two opinions?'..."

1 KINGS 18:21

Have you heard the phrase that the urgent often crowds out the most important? Most people would say that their friends and family members are the most important thing in their lives. Yet work, house projects, and responding to emails often take precedence over these relationships. It's because the urgent crowds out the important time and time again.

The second principle is this...

Principle #2: Urgency fuels Faith or Fear

Urgency is a reality of life. There will always be something that comes up that is urgent. But in your urgency beware. Now is a time when faith will be fueled or fear will be fueled. Our attitude in the midst of urgency determines the fuel we're adding to the fire of our hearts.

Back to 1 Kings 18. Elijah finds himself in an urgent situation. The nation of Israel has all but completely walked away from God and it seems like there may only be a few followers of God left. If he doesn't do something soon, the few followers that are left may even be killed by Ahab, leaving Elijah completely alone.

He says to Ahab and the nation of Israel in 1 Kings 18:21, "How long will you waiver between two opinions?"

Elijah has a conviction and he sees his nation's faith in the balance.

This is what we know about our attitudes in the midst of urgency:
Urgency with conviction fuels faith.
While the opposite fuels fear…
Urgency with apathy fuels fear.

For Elijah, he had the great conviction for his nation to come back around to God. This conviction led him to do the unimaginable. He called for a showdown. A showdown on the top of Mount Carmel to prove whose God truly rules. Tomorrow we'll unpack what this showdown looked like. He invited all the prophets of Baal (a god of the Sidonians) and all the prophets of Asherah (another god worshipped during that time period): 850 of these prophets in all were invited to this showdown. The numbers are definitely not in his favor; 850 prophets to these other gods versus Elijah. But you can see this is the impact of conviction in urgency upon one's faith.

I've also personally witnessed the opposite in people. They find themselves in a crucible moment of life, but their attitude is one of apathy. They are apathetic to life change, they are apathetic to their emotions, they are apathetic to their impact upon others, they are apathetic to injustice, and before you know it their lives are completely ruled by fear.

If you find yourself in the middle of a crisis, but not caring, watch out! Your thoughts will likely lean toward fueling fear. In that moment you need to ask God to cause a conviction to stir up in your heart. The reason is godly conviction will start to breathe life into your faith once again.

Maybe the most basic prayer you can pray today is, "God, stir a conviction in my heart today."

Elijah not only had conviction, he also had a sense of calling to do something about it.

One could say it this way:

Urgency with a sense of unique calling fuels faith.

While…

Urgency without a sense of unique calling fuels fear.

For Elijah saw himself with a unique calling…

In 1 Kings 18:22 he says, "'I am the only one of the LORD's prophets left…'"

He saw himself as one of the only ones who could make a difference here! Most of us could fill in a blank for that. "I'm the only one (or I'm uniquely positioned) to make the difference here…"

- I'm the only teacher at my school that can represent God to the fourth grade.

- I'm the only salesman to represent God in my department.

- I'm the only Christian in my apartment building to represent God to my neighbors.

- I'm the only Christian on my sports team to represent faith in God to my teammates.

Sometimes our aloneness can feel so overwhelming that we feel afraid, but it can also be used in this crucible moment to create urgency around a unique calling to fuel our faith.

Embrace your unique "aloneness, oneness, onlyness" to fuel your faith. This idea that… "If I don't do it, I don't see anyone else who will do it."

Someone has to stand in the gap of injustice, someone has to step up and do what is right, someone has to bring the light where no one else is, and you are that person.

If you feel like you're the only one, that feeling can fuel your fear (because all you see is your aloneness) or it can fuel your faith (because you see your unique calling) in a huge way.

You are the outnumbered Elijah in your setting. And that's not always a bad thing. Perhaps that is because it is the unique place you are called to. May it stir confidence and faith in your life today.

DAILY DISCOVERY: Do you find yourself in the midst of the urgent? Urgency is often the setting of fueling faith or fear. Let's not allow apathy or a sense of aloneness to cause fear. But instead, let's believe big that you and I carry conviction and calling in the midst of the urgency.

SKEPTIC'S CHALLENGE/ PRAYER: What do you carry conviction for in life? Where do you feel like you may be the only one fighting for something? Perhaps a simple prayer might be, *"God, stir a confidence in me around my conviction and solidify a clear calling to make a difference here. May fear have no hold on me."*

NOTES

WEEK SEVEN / DAY FOUR

FAITH VS. FEAR:
THE FUEL OF HONOR AND ATTENTION

31 "Elijah took twelve stones, one for each of the tribes descended from Jacob, to whom the word of the LORD had come, saying, 'Your name shall be Israel.' **32** With the stones he built an altar in the name of the LORD…"

1 KINGS 18:31-32

The showdown that I referred to yesterday was one that required great faith. Remember it was 850 prophets of Baal and Asherah against Elijah. The challenge was this: each group sacrificed a bull to their God. Then they started praying to their God and whichever God sent fire from heaven to burn up the sacrifice would be the God who won and the God that Israel worshipped.

Elijah let the 850 prophets of Baal and Asherah go first. For hours, they danced, prayed, cut themselves with knives, bled everywhere, and nothing happened. As the day turned toward afternoon, Elijah took his turn. First he made quite a display with his altar.

31 "Elijah took twelve stones, one for each of the tribes descended from Jacob, to whom the word of the LORD had come, saying, 'Your name shall be Israel.' **32** With the stones he built an altar in the name of the LORD…"

1 KINGS 18:31-32

Notice what he did: he made this clearly about God and honoring God.

Then, before he started his prayer, he had the prophets dig a trench around his altar. Then he had them fill up massive jars of water and pour them all over the sacrifice, the wood the sacrifice is on, the altar itself, and in the trench.

Finally, his prayer began. As he called out to the God of Israel, without delay, fire fell from heaven and consumed the sacrifice, the wood, the altar itself, and licked up all the water in the trench.

Elijah's faith was on fire (literally fire was falling). But his faith was centered around giving honor and directing all attention to God.

This is the third principle of what fuels Faith or Fear.

Principle #3: What you honor and give attention to fuels Faith or Fear.

When you honor God with your life and give attention to the things of God you will fuel your faith. Conversely, when you honor and give your attention to filth you will fuel your fear.

Question: What type of music do you listen to? What do you watch on TV? What kind of magazines, books, or articles do you read? What news do you listen to? (Are you aware most news is fear oriented?)

What we do is we give our emotions, time, attention, and honor to those things. If after hanging out with your friends and listening to their advice you are more defensive, angry, or fearful, you are probably honoring and giving attention to bad advice.

I'm sure you've heard the phrase "Garbage in, garbage out." It's true whether we are talking about the food we eat, or the type of friends we surround ourselves with, or the music we listen to. What type of fuel are you placing on the fire of your heart? Are you honoring and giving attention to things that will produce fear, or are you honoring and giving your attention to things that will grow your faith and confidence?

DAILY DISCOVERY: Philippians 4:8 says, "Finally, brothers and sisters, whatever is true, whatever is noble, whatever is right, whatever is pure, whatever is lovely, whatever is admirable—if anything is excellent or praiseworthy—think about such things."

Let's make a big move today and make a commitment to try to only think about things that are true, noble, right, pure, lovely, admirable, excellent, or praiseworthy. What do you think God will do in your heart and mind, when those are the only things that get your honor and attention today?

SKEPTIC'S CHALLENGE/ PRAYER: Do you agree with the concept of garbage in, garbage out? What type of fuel are you placing on the fire of your heart? What could it look like today to only allow things into your thinking that are good, admirable, and excellent?

NOTES

WEEK SEVEN / DAY FIVE

FAITH VS. FEAR:
THE FUEL OF MISSION

3 "Elijah was afraid and ran for his life. 4 ...he... went a day's journey into the wilderness. He came to a broom bush, sat down under it and prayed that he might die. 'I have had enough, LORD,' he said. 'Take my life...'"

1 KINGS 19:3-4

Years ago, I decided I wanted to get into racing and triathlons. I always struggled to be consistent in my cardio workouts and I figured if I registered myself for some races I would have to be consistent to get in shape for each race. I was right, that year I was the most consistent in my workouts that I've ever been. When it came time for my first race, it was an off-road triathlon. It consisted of kayaking, mountain biking, and ended with a trail run. Each transition between the three portions of the race took place on a sandy beach.

For kayaking and mountain biking, I pretty much remained in the middle of the pack. However, while heading into the running portion I hadn't noticed it at first, but it became pretty clear that I had gotten sand in my socks. This little bit of sand started as a mild nuisance and because I didn't want to fall behind, I just kept going. But that mild nuisance quickly turned into excruciating pain. I could feel skin being rubbed off and fresh wounds in the making.

I knew I couldn't just keep going with that sand in my socks. So I stopped, took off my socks, got all the sand out, saw my wounds in the process and then put it all back on to finish the race. Unfortunately, the damage was done and every step in my stride became a step of great pain. If it hadn't been for setting my goal and having a mission to finish the race, there is no way I would have kept going. If that had happened on a day that I was just "out for a run" I would have quit. But it wasn't.

It wasn't just a day out for a run, it was a day I had trained for, a day for which I had studied the trail maps, a day where I had a mission. And what I know is true is that even in exhaustion, if you have a mission, you're likely to press on.

This is a great picture of the fourth principle of fueling Faith or Fear:

Principle #4: Your awareness of your mission in the midst of exhaustion fuels Faith or Fear.

Remember Elijah. He just had this amazing victory over 850 false prophets. The nation saw the victory, they are returning to the Lord. Elijah prays that the rain that hadn't come in years returns and that's exactly what happens. The Lord releases a downpour over the land. You would think this is the greatest victory of all time and finally time for Elijah to relax. Unfortunately, Ahab's wife, Jezebel, was a really wicked woman and she was livid. You see, those 850 prophets were her guys and Baal and Asherah were her gods. And now it's all over for those who worship Baal and Asherah. So she sends a threat to Elijah. Her threat is simple. I'm going have you killed within 24 hours.

Elijah just took on 850 false prophets. But the threat of Jezebel pushes him over the edge. Check out what happens next.

3 "Elijah was afraid and ran for his life. 4 ...he... went a day's journey into the wilderness. He came to a broom bush, sat down under it and prayed that he might die. 'I have had enough, LORD,' he said. 'Take my life...'"
1 KINGS 19:3-4

Hold on. When he was facing 850 false prophets he wasn't afraid, but now the threats of one woman cause fear to overtake him?

My argument is this: up until this point, Elijah had a mission. His mission was to see the people return to God. Now his mission is over, he's completely exhausted, and he doesn't necessarily know what to do next. When you're exhausted without a sense of purpose (or mission) you'll often find fear hiding right around the corner.

The first thing is to recognize your exhausted state. Have you ever made a bad decision when you were worn out or exhausted? I have. Just beware that exhaustion ignored and without a mission fuels fear. But exhaustion cared for, with a renewed mission, fuels faith. This is what Elijah needs and this is what God gives to him. The Lord sends an angel to care for him in his exhaustion and then the angel gives Elijah his next mission.

His mission is to travel to another mountain (Mt. Horeb) where he will receive his next assignment. But what the angel does is remind him that he has someplace to go and something to do.

For you, you have some places where the Lord is calling you to go and you have some things you're being called to do.

So if you find yourself exhausted, it's time to take care of yourself and ask God for a renewed mission.

For some of you this might be the most important step you take this week. You need to eat healthier to feel better, go to bed earlier to get enough rest, you need to exercise to feel energized (because in exhaustion we have a tendency to tip toward fear), and then you need to ask God for a renewed mission in your life.

DAILY DISCOVERY: If you're exhausted, let's take two big steps today. First, let's ask God what we need to do to renew our strength (whether that is emotional strength or physical strength). Second, let's make sure we know what our mission is. If you don't have a clear mission right now, ask God to reveal to you what your next step is in your mission.

SKEPTIC'S CHALLENGE/ PRAYER: Write down one thing you know refreshes you when you are exhausted. Second, write down at least one thing that you think could be a part of God's mission for your life right now.

WEEK SEVEN / DAY SIX & SEVEN

What idea was most challenging to you this week?

What day from this week or concept do you want to rethink about?

NOTES

WEEK EIGHT

WEEK EIGHT / DAY ONE

FRUIT VS. FLESH:
THE EXPLORATION OF THE SPIRIT

"For the flesh desires what is contrary to the Spirit, and the Spirit what is contrary to the flesh."

GALATIANS 5:17

"But the fruit of the Spirit is love, joy, peace, patience, kindness, goodness, faithfulness,"

GALATIONS 5:22 (NASB)

Have you ever found yourself in this position? Things are going really well in your day and then something stressful, difficult, or hurtful happens and you find yourself falling to anger or hurtful responses. The worst part is these responses are to the people we love most. As soon as the cutting words come out of your mouth, you completely regret it. Yet you find yourself falling to the works of the flesh.

This area of our identity is one that unfortunately can't fly under the radar. The truth is if you don't carry a royal mindset, most people won't really pick up on that. If you are living in fear over faith, you can fake having a positive attitude in front of people and they may not ever know you're struggling with fear. However, as we consider the principles of the fruit versus flesh, this is the one area of your identity that people will see. You just can't hide it. Like accidentally dying my hair orange in high school. It was the era of frosting your tips, but there was a kid every week who failed to frost just the tips of their hair and instead turned their entire head orange. I was that kid. I walked into class and everyone looked at me and said, "Tried to dye your tips and failed, huh?" "Yep!" I replied. There was just no hiding it.

The reality is, you may be able to fake a lot of things in life, but your spouse, your kids, and your friends know exactly what realm of your identity you're living out and if you're producing fruit versus flesh.

The Bible describes it this way in Galatians:

"For the flesh desires what is contrary to the Spirit, and the Spirit what is contrary to the flesh." GALATIANS 5:17

"But the fruit of the Spirit is love, joy, peace, patience, kindness, goodness, faithfulness," GALATIONS 5:22 (NASB)

When the Bible refers to our flesh, it is referring to our sinful nature that is contrary to the Spirit's nature. So it is not just a neutral response or even just our natural response. It is instead a response that is contrary to God's good, best, and right response in us.

Here's why this matters:

"You, my brothers and sisters, were called to be free. But do not use your freedom to indulge the flesh; rather, serve one another humbly in love." GALATIANS 5:13

You've got to understand, as the Apostle Paul was writing 2,000 years ago and I'm writing today, we're not saying this to heap rules on top of you. This is actually all about living in freedom.

If you've ever been caught in the cycle of sin, or the grip of your flesh, you know you never feel more trapped and dissatisfied as you do when caught in that cycle. The fruit of the Spirit is freedom from a life that is trapped in the cycle of the flesh.

The first principle of producing fruit, not the flesh, is found here in Galatians:

"So I say, walk by the Spirit, and you will not gratify the desires of the flesh." GALATIANS 5:16

The principle is...
Principle #1: The extent that I can walk in the Spirit is determined by how much I explore the Spirit.

Here's why I say "explore the Spirit." The word that gets translated as *walk* in Galatians 5:16 is the Greek word *peripateo*. It can be translated as walk, live, tread around, or walk at large. But it has this idea of purposefully exploring or covering a lot of territory.

I lived in Minnesota for just a couple of years as a young boy. We were lucky to live in a house on a lake surrounded with tons of woods to explore. I remember coming home from school and every day grabbing a quick snack and then heading out to explore, build a fort in the woods, take the canoe across the lake, really do anything to explore the outdoors. Now, as an adult, I wonder how many of my neighbors stared out of their large windows overlooking the woods and the lake and never took the time to explore any of it.

In the same way, many Christians have been told that they can live by the power of the Holy Spirit. They can experience the fruit of the Spirit. But Galatians doesn't tell us to, "gaze out your windows at the Spirit," it says *walk* in the Spirit. And that word is to tread around or walk at large. It's about exploring the Spirit. In a practical sense, this is all about actively listening to the Spirit. It's about trying out new responses as you sense His leading and promptings in your life. It's about looking for His perspective in a situation.

For example, I'll have these moments where I walk into a room that is a complete mess (courtesy of my young kids) and find myself losing my patience. I will feel/ hear the Spirit of God produce almost a "gut check" in me. It's just for a moment, but in that moment I have the opportunity to listen and follow the Spirit who will produce fruit within me, or ignore Him and go with my flesh (which will likely result in me losing my patience as I get overwhelmed by the mess).

Exploring the Spirit is committing to listen to those gut checks—those promptings from the Spirit—and asking God to produce something new within you: fruit.

DAILY DISCOVERY: Our experiment of the day is to believe big that God wants to produce fruit within you. It's a response that apart from Him, you know you wouldn't be able to produce on your own. Today, look and listen for the stirring/prompting from the Spirit. When it happens, ask God what the response is that He wants to produce in you at that moment.

SKEPTIC'S CHALLENGE/ PRAYER: Today's experiment is all about exploring the Spirit. Much like exploring the woods behind my Minnesota home, explore freely. This exploration simply starts with a commitment to look and listen for God's heart, His perspective, and His response throughout your day. It's up to you if you want to step into a different response than your flesh. Just ask God. He may produce some fruit in you that you've never experienced before.

NOTES

WEEK EIGHT / DAY TWO

FRUIT VS. FLESH:
I CAN'T DO WHATEVER I WANT?!

"For the flesh desires what is contrary to the Spirit, and the Spirit what is contrary to the flesh. They are in conflict with each other, so that you are not to do whatever you want."

GALATIANS 5:17

I've probably made the same statement a thousand times to my kids, and I'm sure my parents said it to me as well. That statement is, "When you move out, you can do whatever you want. But as long as you are under my roof..."

It usually follows these types of situations: I tell my child to clean up their room. They say, "I love living in a messy room." And I make the dreaded statement, "When you move out, you can do whatever you want."

They say: I don't want to shower every day.
I say: When you move out, you can do whatever you want.
They say: I don't feel like doing my homework.
I say: When you move out, you can do whatever you want.
They say: I don't want to eat my vegetables.
I say: When you move out, you can do whatever you want.
You get the gist.

While we may say it as a joking statement, nothing could be further from the truth. Even when you move out and are on your own, there are countless things that you cannot do however you want. You can't allow your pet to go to the bathroom in your neighbor's yard, you can't allow your house to fall apart, you can't show up late for work, you can't ignore your relationships, you can't pretend you have a bottomless bank account.

In fact, that mindset is so powerful, if you believe as an adult you can live however you want, it will derail your ability to walk in this area of your identity.

Some of you are so far from the Fruit of what God can produce in you because you so deeply believe, "I'm a grown-up, and I get to do whatever I want."

The truth is, I don't get to do whatever I want, but to walk in freedom and produce fruit, I will do whatever He wants.

Principle #2: I must have the conviction that I don't get to do whatever I want.

Galatians 5:17 says, "For the flesh desires what is contrary to the Spirit, and the Spirit what is contrary to the flesh. They are in conflict with each other, so that you are not to do whatever you want."

The second half of that verse says it plainly, "So that you are not to do whatever you want."

There are many times when what I want is completely driven by my flesh. There are times I just want to explode and yell when my kids aren't listening. (Maybe that will get their attention.) There are times I want to make a comment that will hurt the person just a little bit and let them know how I truly feel. (Maybe that will change their behavior.) There are times I just want to give into temptation. (Maybe that will bring me some happiness.)

Although it's what I want to do, I have to have the conviction that I don't get to do whatever I want. Instead, I want to do whatever He wants me to do. His ways and His responses are fruit. They are healthy. They are good. They are wholesome. They are helpful to others and helpful to myself.

But to step into a fruitful identity, I must acknowledge that I don't get to do whatever I want.

DAILY DISCOVERY: Did you grow up thinking that "someday I'll get to do whatever I want?" How has that led to flesh-driven decisions? Are those decisions and behaviors good and helpful or hurtful and destructive? Throughout the day, let's live from the perspective that it is not always best to do whatever we want, but instead it is always best to do whatever He wants. When you face a hurdle or difficulty today, pause, and don't just respond. Instead, ask God, "How do you want me to respond right now?" And step into a response that is not your way, but His way.

SKEPTIC'S CHALLENGE/ PRAYER: Did you grow up thinking that "Someday I'll get to do whatever I want?" How have these decisions and behaviors been good and helpful or hurtful and destructive? When you face a hurdle or difficulty today, pause, and don't just respond. Instead, consider what response God might have for you. Try not to respond your way, but His way.

NOTES

WEEK EIGHT / DAY THREE

FRUIT VS. FLESH:
THE HONEST ASSESSMENT OF WHAT I'M
PRODUCING

18 "But if you are led by the Spirit, you are not under the law. 19 The acts of the flesh are obvious: sexual immorality, impurity and debauchery;"

GALATIANS 5:18-19

14 "As obedient children, do not conform to the evil desires you had when you lived in ignorance. 15 But just as he who called you is holy, so be holy in all you do;"

1 PETER 1:14-15

With nine kids, we have experienced a handful of times when they struggled with their grades at school. It amazed me how often the conversation went the same way. We sat the child down to talk through what they were doing and they responded by saying, "I'm doing all that I can do." Well, that's never true. There is usually some homework that could be made up, a test that could be retaken, or some extra credit that could be done to raise the grade. But their perspective is almost always, "I'm doing all that I can do." Their problem is that they are not being honest with themselves or their actions that have brought them this far. And if they don't own up to the fact that there is something that must be done differently, they will continue down the same path. Unfortunately that path is a path toward failing a class.

Often we do the same in life; we continue to "fail" in an area of our life, but we are so hard-hearted we are not willing to be honest about the pain we are causing ourselves or others.

The third principle of the Fruit vs. Flesh speaks into this.

Principle #3: Take an honest assessment of what I am currently producing.

1 Peter 1:14 says, "As obedient children, do not conform to the evil desires you had when you lived in ignorance."

You and I can't keep playing the ignorance card. Those who live by the flesh apart from Christ do so in ignorance. If you don't claim to have a relationship with God, then quite frankly, you're off the hook here. But if you do claim to be a Christian, you have to be honest with yourself and take an honest assessment of your actions.

We've all grown up hearing the phrase, "Everyone is doing it." Maybe you even said that to your parents. If you did, your parents probably responded by saying, "If everyone jumped off a cliff, would you follow them?"

While that sounds so extreme, Christians are still constantly, foolishly, using that argument as to why they are living in sin or condoning sin in others by saying, "Everyone else is doing it."

While I can't be mad at someone without the Spirit of God living in a rebellious way, I also shouldn't use their moral compass as my standard.

I can't be mad if culture doesn't have a moral compass built on the Bible. But I can be mad if Christians don't.

Galatians 5:19-21 says, 19 "The acts of the flesh are obvious: sexual immorality, impurity [this is the Greek word porneia, it's where we get the word porn from] and debauchery; 20 idolatry and witchcraft; hatred, discord, jealousy, fits of rage, selfish ambition, dissensions, factions 21 and envy; drunkenness, orgies, and the like. I warn you, as I did before, that those who live like this will not inherit the kingdom of God."

He's saying these are the activities that show that one is not a child of God.

If you are regularly participating in some of these activities, either you are not a Christian—in which case God's heart is to save you from that cycle of bondage (and He loves you so much He sent His Son to lay down His life for you to pay for your sins)—or you are a child of God living in rebellion, caught deep in the cycle of your flesh.

On the other hand, Galatians 5:22-23 says, 22 "But the fruit of the Spirit is love, joy, peace, forbearance, kindness, goodness, faithfulness, 23 gentleness and self-control..."

What are you producing? The Flesh or Fruit?

Either way, the principle here is that we can't live in ignorance any longer. It's time to get honest with ourselves.

DAILY DISCOVERY: Today let's make it our goal to be entirely honest with ourselves and God. This is a big task, but here's the goal: all throughout your day, make constant assessments of your responses. Simply ask, "Was my thought pattern, my response, or my behavior from the flesh or the fruit of the Spirit?" The more we are purposeful to identify what is being produced in us, the more opportunity we have to bring our thoughts, our responses, and our behaviors in line with God's desires.

SKEPTIC'S CHALLENGE/ PRAYER: Even if you don't have a relationship with God, you can be honest with yourself about your thought patterns, your responses, and your behaviors. Do you like them? Are they fulfilling or are they draining? Do you wish you would handle situations differently at times? Reread Galatians 5:22-23. What fruit from that list do you wish you carried more of? I would challenge you to ask God to give you some of it today.

WEEK EIGHT / DAY FOUR

FRUIT VS. FLESH:
WHAT IS ALIVE AND WHAT IS DEAD?

"Those who belong to Christ Jesus have crucified the flesh with its passions and desires."

GALATIANS 5:24

One of my favorite shows to watch is "Alone." It's a reality show that drops 10 people out in the wilderness and they simply survive for as long as they can, alone. The person who lasts the longest gets a half million dollars. Often the survivalists are dropped in wilderness settings where they encounter some aggressive wildlife. On most occasions, bears are a predator on their land. If you've ever lived in bear country you probably know what to do when wandering the woods. You see it displayed in almost every episode of "Alone." People are walking through the woods just randomly yelling, "Hey bear!" They are doing it purposefully in an effort to scare away any bears in the area. They also do it because they never want to randomly come across a bear and frighten it. That would likely result in a bear attack. Their declarations bring them confidence and remind the bear to stay away.

In the same way, we actually need to do the same. We need to declare what we intend to produce in our lives. In doing so we can set ourselves up to produce fruit and remind the flesh to stay away.

The fourth principle of Fruit vs. Flesh is:

Principle #4: I remind myself of what is alive and what is dead.

"Those who belong to Christ Jesus have crucified the flesh with its passions and desires." **GALATIANS 5:24**

For Christians this means that our flesh is technically dead. Meaning, fruit is actually what is alive and is meant to be produced in you.

When I remind myself what is dead, I'm also reminding my enemy (the devil) that my thought processes, my responses, and my behaviors no longer belong to him. It's like I'm shouting in the woods, "Hey Bear!" But I'm shouting over my heart, "The flesh is dead and fruit is alive in me."

I find that I have to remind my heart and mind of my fruitful identity often.

Like all of us, I face things in life that cause fear to rear its ugly head. When I find fear taking ahold of my heart and mind, I remind myself that fear is my flesh response. I quote out loud 2 Timothy 1:7 that says, "The Lord has not given me a spirit of fear or timidity, but of power, love, and self-discipline."

There is something so powerful in the declaration of your true identity. Remind yourself what is alive in you today.

DAILY DISCOVERY: Yesterday you took the time to do some honest assessments of your thoughts, attitudes, and behaviors. Today, put your faith into action by declaring over yourself what is truly dead and what is truly alive. Remind your heart and mind that the flesh was crucified with Christ, meaning it died with Christ at the cross. Now you are a child of God filled with the fruit of God.

SKEPTIC'S CHALLENGE/ PRAYER: Have you ever found yourself stuck in a bad cycle? Have you wanted out, tried to get out and simply felt stuck? If there truly is a better way of living, ask God to give you a vision or image of what life could be like with the flesh dead and the fruit of God alive in you.

WEEK EIGHT / DAY FIVE

FRUIT VS. FLESH: TAKING A STRATEGIC STEP

"Since we live by the Spirit, let us keep in step with the Spirit."

GALATIANS 5:25

I have three apple trees in my backyard. Unfortunately, we rarely enjoy any apples from those trees. Some years around harvest time we may find a few apples that are worthy of eating. But most years the apples are eaten by bugs or critters or the trees don't even produce for whatever reason. I wish my apple trees produced good fruit, however, I can't be mad that they don't because I don't do anything to help them produce fruit. I don't trim them, I don't spray them, I don't water them, I don't care for them. I do nothing.

Many Christians are the same. They want to see God grow them and produce fruit in them, but they are unwilling to do anything to help make that happen. They don't take a single strategic step toward growth and then wonder why they struggle in this battle between their flesh and the fruit of the Spirit.

The fifth principle of Fruit vs. Flesh will speak into this:

Principle #5: We must take a strategic step to walk with the Spirit.

Galatians 5:25 says, "Since we live by the Spirit, let us keep in step with the Spirit."

The word that gets translated as "keep in step" is the Greek word *stoicheo*, which means to walk orderly, to march as a soldier, or to go in order. This is not meandering through life with God, but a strategic type of walking that is being described.

If you want to get in shape physically, the first thing most people are going to do is get a plan. A plan gives us a strategy for how we will exercise daily, eat better, get a full night's sleep, etc. In the same way we cannot just hope to become people who produce the fruit of the Spirit; we need a plan.

God gives us an insight into how to produce this fruit through strategic steps that we take to walk with Him. Like a soldier who marches in perfect step with a cadence, similarly we need to take purposeful steps to walk in the cadence of God in our lives. This won't happen through hoping to live better or wishing to be better. It will happen with strategic steps.

By working your way through this book you are doing that. You are strategically reading scripture, processing your faith, and seeking God. But for many of us there are some additional steps that we can take to strategically walk us toward freedom from the patterns of the flesh.

Celebrate Recovery is an awesome group we offer at our church (and is offered at churches across the nation) to help people take a strategic step toward freedom. If not CR, consider a small group, an online group, or a similar opportunity at a local church. Read your Bible daily, pray daily, process this book with others on a weekly basis. But do something strategic.

Have you ever thought to yourself that you wanted to go on a diet, but you only thought and never said it to anyone? Because as soon as you say it, now there is a level of accountability toward the goal. Sometimes our first strategic step in faith is the same way. You need to just say it, to cause a level of accountability toward it.

You'll never see God produce the fruit He wants to produce in you, unless you strategically take steps in that direction. Say it and take the step.

DAILY DISCOVERY: Do you want to see change in your life? Today, let's take a big and bold step toward real change. Reach out to a local Celebrate Recovery group, consider joining a small group at a church, or tell someone about the accountability you want in your life. Continue to follow up on those steps, because they will lead you toward walking in step with Him and ultimately producing His fruit.

SKEPTIC'S CHALLENGE/ PRAYER: Do you want to see change in your life? Today, let's take a big and bold step toward real change. Reach out to a local Celebrate Recovery group, consider joining a small group at a church, or tell someone about the accountability you want in your life. Continue to follow up on those steps, because they will lead you toward walking in step with Him and ultimately producing His fruit.

NOTES

WEEK EIGHT / DAY SIX & SEVEN

DAY 6: LET THAT THOUGHT SIMMER

What idea was most challenging to you this week?

DAY 7: LET THAT THOUGHT SIMMER

What day from this week or concept do you want to rethink about?

ESTABLISHING YOUR IDENTITY

WEEK NINE

WEEK NINE / DAY ONE

ADOPTED VS. ORPHANED: CONFIDENT OR INSECURE

"he predestined us for adoption to sonship through Jesus Christ, in accordance with his pleasure and will—"

EPHESIANS 1:5

Do you remember the show "Sesame Street" and its "One Of These Things Doesn't Belong" segment? They would have three people doing one activity like jump roping and then one person doing something entirely different like hula hooping, and sing this song stating, "One of these things is not like the other, one of these things doesn't belong." For some reason I always felt bad for the one thing that didn't belong. Unfortunately there are many people who feel like the odd man out in life. They feel like they don't belong even in the family of faith. This week we are going to be anchored in the belief of belonging, specifically how that can play out in an adopted versus orphaned spirit.

To help see the difference between the two, I would say it this way:

Orphaned mindset: was not a part of the family, but now lives with a family, but **does not belong** to the family.

Adopted mindset: was not part of the family, but now lives with the family, and **belongs** to the family.

In Ephesians 1:5 it says, "he predestined us for adoption to sonship through Jesus Christ, in accordance with his pleasure and will—"

The Apostle Paul is describing the entrance process into this family of God. It says he's adopted us to sonship. Sometimes in the Bible, the Greek word that gets translated as "sons" can equally be translated as "children" as it's really not gender-specific. In which case most Bible translations will translate it "sons and daughters" or "children." However in this case, it is specifically "sonship" vs. children.

Here's why it matters in this passage, matters in the culture, and matters to us. In those days the inheritance always went to the oldest son, and if he wasn't around, then to the next oldest, then the next, etc. It's important that as children of God we understand this. What we receive is the inheritance of the eldest son. What's crazy here is that the idea that an adopted child would receive the inheritance as if they were a son was unheard of 2,000 years ago. In fact, people might be kind and invite someone to live with them and care for them, but they would not go through the legal process of adoption for this very reason. They would not want their estate and inheritance to pass to anyone outside of the bloodline and immediate family. But what God is saying here is that God not only wants us to be with Him and be cared for by Him, but He also wants to give us the full inheritance of Jesus.

His desire is to adopt you into the family, to receive the greatest inheritance level He offers, and He is happy to do it.

If you wouldn't call yourself a Christian, I'm glad you're still in this God experiment. Today what I want for you is to know what God intends to hand out (the liberation He wants for His children).

We're going to look at five contrasting Adopted vs. Orphaned mindsets. The first is:

Principle #1: An Adopted mindset has independent (or personal) confidence while an Orphaned mindset competes and needs to stand out.

Those who feel like spiritual orphans, because they don't feel accepted, feel the need to prove their worth or make a statement with their life to stand out.

Acts 10:34-35 says, 34 "Then Peter began to speak: 'I now realize how true it is that God does not show favoritism 35 but accepts from every nation the one who fears him and does what is right.'"

What does it mean that God does not show favoritism but accepts from every nation equally? It means there is nothing that you or I could do to edge our way up into greater favor with God to receive more love from Him, more acceptance from Him, more grace from Him, or more inheritance from Him.

If you carry an orphaned mindset, these are some of the traits you might exhibit:

You seek to hide your own limitations.
You perceive the strength of others as competition.
You secretly take satisfaction in the weakness of others.
You need and seek attention.

But those who are confident in their adoption and belief of belonging embrace both their strengths and weaknesses, and are comfortable with who they are and whose they are.

They don't jockey for position and recognition.

They cover each other's weaknesses and joyfully add their combined strengths to the family.

In our home, with our nine kids, we hear a phrase used by our kids quite often. It was originally coined by my oldest daughter and it has kind of become a joke in the house. It's "What about me?" We hear it anytime either Lisa or I give a compliment to one of our children in front of the others. I'll say, "Way to go on getting an A on your test," to one child and all the other children will say, "What about me?" I'll say, "You did an awesome job cleaning your room," to one and all the others will say, "What about me?" It's like we can't give a compliment without all the others wanting to receive the same compliment or another of equal praise. While it is always said in a joking way and we all laugh together, there are many who truly perceive God that way.

How many of us truly can't handle someone else in the family of God doing well and receiving God's great blessing upon them without asking,

"What about me"?

Do you ever secretly think about how to make yourself stand out from the other children in the family to somehow be a favorite child?

Do you ever feel like you're competing with other Christians to be the "best" Christian, to earn the favorite child award?

This is actually an orphaned mindset.

DAILY DISCOVERY: Let's live today with a strong adopted mindset, confident in who you are and whose you are. Today, look for someone else who has received God's special blessing over them recently (e.g. they got the raise, the new house, the newborn, the healing, etc.). Take some time to celebrate that with them. Honor God and give Him thanks for His blessing in their life. We can do this with confidence, knowing that God does not show favoritism and His blessings will be seen in your life in His perfect timing.

SKEPTIC'S CHALLENGE/ PRAYER: Have you ever tried to live your life to try to win God's approval or acceptance? Have you ever felt like you needed to jockey for God's love? The starting point of understanding the beauty of the family of God is that none of us is more deserving than another to receive God's love, forgiveness, or inheritance. Can you take the day to simply imagine your life through the lens of belonging? If you've never felt like you belong anywhere in the world, this is what God came to remedy.

NOTES

WEEK NINE / DAY TWO

ADOPTED VS. ORPHANED: INTERDEPENDENT OR INDEPENDENT

"Consequently, you are no longer foreigners and strangers, but fellow citizens with God's people and also members of his household."

EPHESIANS 2:19

I've got quite a few friends who have adopted or fostered children over the years. I've heard some interesting stories about some of these kids and some very interesting insights that their behaviors reveal about orphaned or abandoned children. For example, one family told me of a foster child who would take milk and hide it in their closet, or take meat and cheese from the refrigerator and put it under their bed. The child didn't understand that the items would spoil, but they carried the perspective of having to fend for themselves in life. They did not yet carry the mindset that as family, "everything is ours."

In Ephesians 2, the Apostle Paul is describing the family of God this way: "...you are no longer foreigners and strangers, but fellow citizens with God's people and also members of his household." If we are members of His household, we are not alone. Let that sink in for a moment. Earlier we talked about how God never leaves us and we are never alone. While I believe that is true, this is speaking from another perspective. This is the perspective that as members of the same family we never go it alone. You always have a family or a team to rely on.

The second principle of the Adopted versus Orphaned mindset is...

Principle #2: An Adopted mindset approaches things as a family (or team) while an Orphaned mindset approaches things in isolation/ independently (or alone).

Here's how the orphaned spirit may be seen:

Deep down the orphan does not feel as though he or she belongs
in the family.

They suffer from a sense of abandonment.

The instinct of an orphan is to go it alone.

This may result in withdrawal from others, physically and/or
emotionally.

They carry an attitude of independence or self-preservation.

Their personal trust is placed only in themselves.

One of the hurdles that many people face is their own personal history
and relational experiences. If you have any number of years in life
under your belt, you have probably experienced a close friendship or
even family relationship coming to a painful demise. Most of us will
experience either a drifting away of a relationship, or worse: rejection,
betrayal, or abandonment. These experiences cause deep wounds in the
realm of our trust with others. We sometimes come to bad conclusions
that we are the only ones we can rely on and trust in life. This results in
a life of isolation.

Now spiritually translate that into the family of God and you've got quite
a mess. We have a ton of children who carry orphaned mindsets and
don't trust one another. They truly live lives of independence.

Conversely, sons and daughters who understand a healthy view of their
adoption embrace interdependence. They recognize their need for each
other and celebrate being joined together as a family and working as a
team.

A few years ago we were out as a family, shopping. As we were driving
out of the parking lot, my daughter (who was nine at the time), saw
another family coming out of the store and she remarked, "Oh, I feel so
bad for them." To which Lisa responded, "Why do you feel bad for them?"
And she replied, "Because they have such a small family."

Now the truth is, they were probably an average family. We are just an abnormally enormous family. But my daughter (who is our middle child) has never known anything other than a large family.

Don't misunderstand me, there is nothing wrong with small families, she was just responding from her perspective of a large family as it has many hands to help out, many people to do life with, many kids to play with, and many who are a part of the team.

No matter what size biological family you come from, God's spiritual family is a large family. And while we are a bunch of adopted kids, we belong to this large, eclectic, and diverse family. The key here is you belong. If I could give you a principle for belonging it would be this: Belief of abandonment breeds isolation, while the belief of acceptance breeds interdependence.

Do you have a tendency to isolate and go it alone? Or press into and rely on family?

DAILY DISCOVERY: The experiment is this: lean fully into the family of God today. Consider how you and your gifts might be able to offer help or support to someone else in the family. Consider a need you have and don't be afraid to ask someone to help you out, such as with a physical item that you need, or help with a project, etc.

SKEPTIC'S CHALLENGE/ PRAYER: Do you have a tendency to go it alone in life? What appeals to you about leaning into a family who works as a team? Consider how God might want to strengthen you through others around you in life. You could even ask God to bring someone into your life who would help strengthen you.

WEEK NINE / DAY THREE

ADOPTED VS. ORPHANED: DIGNITY OR SHAME

"Both the one who makes people holy [referring to Jesus] and those who are made holy [referring to believers in Christ] are of the same family. So Jesus is not ashamed to call them brothers and sisters."

HEBREWS 2:11

I grew up in a pretty clean-cut Christian family, in the church era when the phrase "Sunday Best" was firmly established. On Sundays families dressed their best, looked their best, and carried themselves to their best ability, but in the end who knows how they truly lived and looked the rest of the week. There is nothing wrong with looking nice, but it seemed like an outward facade that never mattered to me.

So on the day I drove to Indiana to get a tattoo (because I couldn't get one in Illinois at age 18), I knew I was going to push against the stereotypical mindset that nice Christian boys don't grow their hair long or get tattoos. I had already broken the long hair stereotype in high school, so why not get the tattoo now?

I remember the day I showed my dad my new tattoo. It was months later, but his facial response will probably always be burned in my memory. He just hung his head in disappointment and shame. Now, that may not have been exactly what he was feeling, but that was my perception at the time. We've all been there. We have probably all done something in our lives when we thought we brought shame upon the family.

Unfortunately, I think many of us carry that perspective into our spiritual journey and have the perspective that God might have let us into the family, but He's ashamed that we're here. That perspective couldn't be further from the truth.

Hebrews 2:11 says, "Both the one who makes people holy [referring to Jesus] and those who are made holy [referring to believers in Christ] are of the same family. So Jesus is not ashamed to call them brothers and sisters."

Do you see it? He is not ashamed of us. I know there are plenty of things in our lives that probably should cause us shame in the presence of a holy God, yet He says there is no shame for us. The reason for this is because all of our shame was placed on Jesus at the cross.

The third principle of the Adopted vs. Orphaned mindset is:

Principle #3: An Adopted mindset believes in their own personal dignity while an Orphaned mindset believes they are a shame to the family.

We see an interesting moment in the garden of Eden in the book of Genesis. Adam and Eve have sinned when they eat of the fruit of the tree of the knowledge of good and evil. The very first thing they notice after their sin is that they feel shame from their nakedness. And the very first thing God does for them after they sin is He clothes them to cover their nakedness. What is God doing? God is showing grace to cover them and their shame and restore to them a sense of dignity.

The belonging principle is this: Allow your shame to be placed on the cross and clothe yourself in the dignity God has bestowed upon you.

Some of you have felt like you're the black sheep in the family of God. Like God may have allowed you into the family, but most days He's regretting it and carries a lot of shame because of who you are. But just like God took care of Adam and Eve's shame, He's done the same for you and me. At the cross God made a way to cover our shame and clothe us with dignity.

You can carry dignity or shame, but you can't carry both, and your shame was already carried to the cross.

If all your shame was carried to the cross, what is it that you are carrying around which you call shame? That thing you're carrying is an orphaned spirit.

THE ORPHANED SPIRIT:
- feels ashamed
- feels constantly unworthy

ADOPTED SONS AND DAUGHTERS:
- have nothing to fear, as they are secure in their Father's love and place in the family
- find their dignity in the family DNA and who Christ has made them to be
- belong to a family of dignity

DAILY DISCOVERY: The first big step of faith for many is to simply declare over ourselves Hebrews 2:11. Jesus is not ashamed to call me brother or sister. Whatever shame you think you need to carry, take some time to leave it at the foot of the cross, recognizing all your shame was dealt with over 2,000 years ago. Today, carry yourself with the greatest dignity you ever have.

SKEPTIC'S CHALLENGE/ PRAYER: Why do you think God would be ashamed of you? Do you carry yourself as an individual of shame or dignity? How does a kingdom identity of dignity sound to you? Consider asking God to give you a glimpse into the dignity He wants to bestow upon you, when you enter into His family.

NOTES

WEEK NINE / DAY FOUR

ADOPTED VS. ORPHANED: ACCEPTED OR PERFORMANCE ORIENTED

[8] "For it is by grace you have been saved, through faith—and this is not from yourselves, it is the gift of God— [9] not by works, so that no one can boast."

EPHESIANS 2:8-9

I've seen an interesting response from my kids countless times. Lisa and I will tell them we are going to do something fun, such as a bonfire with s'mores after dinner. Immediately after dinner one child says, "Let's get our kitchen chores done quickly so we can go do the bonfire." They all hop out of their chairs with smiles on their faces and quickly get to work. Multiple times when they pass by, they give me a hug, or simply say, "You're the best."

Now, I think it is their excitement of the good thing that is coming their way that causes them to be so overly obedient, helpful, and complimentary. But in many ways it's like they are behaving in such a way to earn the good thing that is coming to them. The truth is they are going to experience the bonfire and s'mores regardless of what they do. But perhaps it's like they want to be deserving of the fun activity.

Spiritually, we unintentionally do the same thing all the time. We know there is nothing that we can do to earn salvation or to be worthy of God's grace, yet somehow we fall to an orphaned mindset that believes we need to work for it and somehow become deserving of God's grace.

An orphan, because they don't have a place in the family, is always trying to earn grace, favor, or position with anyone they encounter. They are performance-oriented individuals.

This is the fourth principle of an Adopted vs. Orphaned mindset:

Principle #4: An Adopted mindset has an acceptance orientation while an Orphaned mindset has a performance orientation.

[8] "For it is by grace you have been saved, through faith—and this is not from yourselves, it is the gift of God— [9] not by works..." EPHESIANS 2:8-9

Not by works! Meaning, there is nothing we can add to the work of the cross to make us more worthy of forgiveness.

An orphaned spirit performs for acceptance while the adopted spirit receives acceptance. This is the difference between working for (trying to earn) the cross versus accepting the work of the cross.

Someone with an orphaned mindset feels rejected—therefore believing that he or she must compensate by working hard or performing well to somehow earn God's love and maintain his or her place in the family.

Sons and daughters generously extend grace to others when they fail to measure up to actual or perceived standards. This is because they know the fullness of the Father's grace toward them.

An area where this really plays out is in one's view and approach to sin. It's the difference between, "How far can I go before I'm disobedient?" and "How can I walk in obedience?"

Another way of saying it is, are you more concerned about breaking God's rules or are you more concerned about honoring your heavenly Father?

Orphaned kids just want to know the household rules so they can go as far up to the edge of those rules as possible without breaking them and getting kicked out. Adopted kids are concerned about family values and honoring those values because they are confident of their place in the family.

Here's how I've seen it play out time and time again. In high school ministry, kids always asked the question, "How far is too far" (sexually speaking)? Often it was because they simply wanted to know how far they could go before they would be breaking God's rules. I would always respond to them through the lens of honoring God and they would always push back through the lens of rules.

The problem is they carried an orphaned mindset. Orphans are rule-based, performance-based thinkers who are only concerned with the do's and don'ts. Adopted kids are acceptance-based thinkers and are concerned with living in a way that honors the adoptive family who has accepted them into their home.

Orphans see God's standard as His standard, His rules and His values.

Adopted children see God's standard, rules, and values as their standard, their rules, and their values which are meant to be fought for and honored.

So instead of pushing the limits to see how close we can get before we break them, we fight hard to honor those standards and even honor the core foundation as to why they exist.

How about you? Are you more concerned about the do's and don'ts or do you want to live in an honoring way to God because you love Him and are a part of the family?

DAILY DISCOVERY: Have you struggled in life with crossing a line into sin (such as exploding in anger)? Instead of looking at the line that shouldn't be crossed; what is the core value of God that established the line in the first place? Maybe it's integrity, purity, patience, kindness, bestowing dignity, etc. Today, instead of trying to not cross the line, let's be the adopted kids who fight for our Father's value system. If it's that you lose your patience to anger, then today exercise your faith in a huge way and believe that you are the greatest ambassador of patience that lives on the planet. Apply this tactic to whatever you've been struggling with. This time approach it as an adopted child, not a spiritual orphan.

SKEPTIC'S CHALLENGE/ PRAYER: Have you looked at God as one who just has a bunch of rules and a list of do's and don'ts? How does your perspective of God change if you know that performance is not a part of the equation with God at all?

NOTES

WEEK NINE / DAY FIVE

ADOPTED VS. ORPHANED: DISCIPLINED OR UNDISCIPLINED

5 "And have you completely forgotten this word of encouragement that addresses you as a father addresses his son? It says,

'My son, do not make light of the Lord's discipline,

and do not lose heart when he rebukes you,

6 because the Lord disciplines the one he loves,

and he chastens everyone he accepts as his son.'"

HEBREWS 12:5-6

29 "Are not two sparrows sold for a penny? Yet not one of them will fall to the ground outside your Father's care. 30 And even the very hairs of your head are all numbered. 31 So don't be afraid; you are worth more than many sparrows."

MATTHEW 10:29-31

I know I talked about my home life growing up as being pretty clean cut and put together. While it felt a little "too perfect" at times, I'm truly so grateful for my parents and my upbringing. Drugs and alcohol weren't a part of my family. Yelling and screaming weren't a part of my family. Abandonment or a lack of care wasn't a part of my family. Swearing or name calling, hitting or abuse, anger or lack of patience, gossip or slander… none of these things were a part of my upbringing. In fact, my parents made it to almost all of my games, recitals, concerts, shows, and big life events. They were also highly involved in my friend choices, grades, good decisions, bad decisions, relationships, discipline as necessary, and so on. The point is, they were fully present in my life. They were fully present pushing me in ways that I liked and ways that I didn't like, but all of that was because they cared about me and had my best interests in mind.

Spiritually speaking, your heavenly Father is "all in" on your life. He is fully present and wants to be involved like an involved parent might want to be. Yes, it may seem like God is always in your space and in your life, but this is because He cares about you and has your best interests in mind.

The fifth principle of the Adopted versus Orphaned mindset is:

Principle #5: An Adopted mindset embraces correction and care while an Orphaned mindset resists God's involvement and behaves undisciplined and abandoned.

In Hebrews 12, the author describes God's involvement in our lives. In these verses, His involvement is not always enjoyable, but it is necessary and it is for our good. It says, "the LORD disciplines the one he loves."

As a parent I now fully understand this. I discipline my kids not because it's fun for me to do so, but because I love them and I want to see them develop to be the best individuals they can be.

Matthew 10:29-31 reminds us how much God cares for us as well. He knows the number of hairs on your head, He knows your every need, and He wants to be present in your life, caring for you.

The belonging principle here is an Adopted spirit expects Fatherly involvement while an Orphaned spirit assumes God is distant and uninterested.

God demonstrates his care by inserting Himself into our lives, bringing correction and discipline because He has not abandoned us.

An Orphan mentality:
- defaults to thinking God doesn't really care that much about being involved in his or her life

- believes God is really busy and his or her needs are low on His list of importance

An Adopted son or daughter:

- expects parental involvement

- expects God's discipline and accepts it, looking for growth through the experience

- expects God to care about all aspects of their life and seeks God's direction in those aspects

Do you believe God is highly interested in being involved in your life, or do you think He is uninterested and too busy? Do you resist God's correction in your life or do you embrace it as a season of growth? Your answers may reveal if you've carried an Adopted or Orphaned mindset.

There is a powerful moment in the middle of the movie "Solo," which is the backstory to the character Han Solo from the *Star Wars* movie series. Han is trying to escape the planet he is on, as well as his small-time smuggling life, and sees an opportunity to join the empire as a fighter pilot. As he is registering, they ask for his name, and he replies, "Han." The officer asks, "Han what? Who are your people?" Han responds, "I don't have any people." The officer looks at Han, thinks for a moment, and then creates an identity for Han right there on the spot and types "Han Solo."

Han continues to live his life under that identity: undisciplined, pushing against all the rules, and isolated because he does life alone, he belongs to no one; he lives life solo.

Unfortunately, there are many Christians who have not fully grasped the concept that you are no longer solo. You are not alone. You have been adopted. It's time to put down the orphaned spirit and pick up your identity as an adopted child of God.

DAILY DISCOVERY: Where do you sense God is presently working in your life? Is it in the area of discipline or care? Let's believe today that God has your best interest in mind. Sometimes His involvement in our lives feels good and sometimes it feels bad, but it is always for our best. Let's carry the Adopted spirit that embraces His involvement and care.

SKEPTIC'S CHALLENGE/ PRAYER: Have you ever thought God doesn't care that much about your life? Or that God is too busy with more important matters or people to be involved in your life? Today, why not explore the idea that God might actually want to be involved in your life? Explore the idea that God might care about all of your passions, interests, questions, doubts, hurts, joys, and even the number of hairs on your head.

NOTES

WEEK NINE / DAY SIX & SEVEN

DAY 6: LET THAT THOUGHT SIMMER

What idea was most challenging to you this week?

DAY 7: LET THAT THOUGHT SIMMER

What day from this week or concept do you want to rethink about?

WEEK TEN

WEEK TEN / DAY ONE

SERVANT LEADER VS. LORDING LEADER: GETTING OUR HANDS DIRTY

"Sitting down, Jesus called the Twelve and said, 'Anyone who wants to be first must be the very last, and the servant of all.'"

MARK 9:35

Let me give you two quick scenarios. One, a neighborhood kid tells another he has to take a drink of beer if he wants to be cool. Surrounded by a growing crowd of kids, he starts to chide, "Are you a scaredy cat?" Two, a teenager kneels down beside his younger sibling who is staring at a bedroom floor covered with toys. The teen says to the young sibling, "Let me help you clean this up, I bet together we can finish it quickly."

In both scenarios we have leaders and we have kids who will be following. Both have forms of influence. The reality is leadership exists in healthy and unhealthy ways even at a very young age. I would argue that we all have a leadership capacity and we all lead something and someone.

BIG IDEA OF LEADERSHIP: We all can and have influence. How we influence will reveal our identity as either a Servant Leader or Lording Leader.

What are the things at the core of our identity that start to dictate how we will lead or how we influence? Are there best practices for leadership?

I want to make the argument that Jesus gave us the best model of leadership and how to influence. That leadership model was as a servant leader. Jesus said this to his disciples in Mark 9:

"Sitting down, Jesus called the Twelve and said, 'Anyone who wants to be first must be the very last, and the servant of all.'" MARK 9:35

Jesus repeatedly spoke about serving others and he modeled serving others until his dying breath on the cross where he gave His life to serve humanity.

As we dive into the subject of our identity as leaders, I believe this week's subject applies to all of us. Christian or non-Christian, I believe we will all be able to take an honest look at our identity as leaders and glean some practical leadership insights. I think we will intuitively be able to recognize the leadership traits that are better for all of us.

The first principle of the Servant Leader vs. the Lording Leader is:

Principle #1: Servant Leaders are not afraid to get their hands dirty. Lording Leaders see themselves as above the fray.

On the final night of Jesus' life, before He went to the cross, He shared a meal with his disciples. That meal, the Last Supper, became the model of why we practice communion today. But before the meal, Jesus did something profound. In those days a common practice when entering into a home was to have your feet washed. This was usually the job of the lowest servant, simply because it was a gross and humbling job. Getting on your knees and washing the filth off the feet of people in that day and age... who knows what they walked through?

Yet Jesus models something in this moment: he takes the place of the lowest servant and washes all 12 disciples' feet. This is how that moment came to a close:

12 "When he had finished washing their feet, he put on his clothes and returned to his place. 'Do you understand what I have done for you?' he asked them. 13 'You call me 'Teacher' and 'LORD,' and rightly so, for that is what I am. 14 Now that I, your LORD and Teacher, have washed your feet, you also should wash one another's feet. 15 I have set you an example that you should do as I have done for you. 16 Very truly I tell you, no servant is greater than his master, nor is a messenger greater than the one who sent him. 17 Now that you know these things, you will be blessed if you do them.'" JOHN 13:12-17

This really cuts straight to the heart of servant leadership. When we say servant leadership, the model Christ gives us is a leader who is humble, who is not afraid to get His hands dirty, who is not too important or too great to serve the very people who are there to serve Him.

Whenever I finish up a one-on-one conversation with one of my staff members, I usually end that conversation by asking, "Is there anything I can do for you?" I learned to ask that simple question from my observations of another leader. But it's a simple exchange that reminds my heart of the leader I'm meant to be and the type of leader I want them to become.

At some point in your life you've probably had to work for someone or follow someone who was a Lording Leader. You've probably seen someone model the idea of "Don't get your hands dirty, and as soon as you can pass the least desired jobs to someone else, do so."

Do you lead that way? Do you look forward to passing off the worst jobs to the newbies in your sphere of influence? Or do you look for ways to serve those who are there to serve you?

DAILY DISCOVERY: Today let's get our hands dirty. Not just for the sake of nostalgia, but truly wanting to come alongside those we influence. Instead of barking out orders, let's invite someone to join us in a place where we can bring influence.

SKEPTIC'S CHALLENGE/ PRAYER: What type of leadership have you observed more of throughout your life, a lording leader or a servant leader? What do you think you lean toward? If you've never put on the identity of a servant leader, try it today (get your hands dirty) and really look for the supernatural and divine ways this perspective can change you and those you lead.

WEEK TEN / DAY TWO

SERVANT LEADER VS. LORDING LEADER: DEVELOPING OTHERS

"I have set you an example that you should do as I have done for you."
JOHN 13:15

I was recently talking with a colleague who had left their previous job within the year and had started a new job. When I asked what happened that caused them to move on, their response was, "I just felt like a pawn in their system, always being dictated to and moved from place to place without input from me."

As a leader, I understand there are times that tough decisions have to be made, people and positions need to be moved, but how we handle that process matters. How we lead through those seasons matters.

Yesterday we looked at how Jesus modeled servant leadership in a beautiful display when He washed His disciples' feet. After he had washed their feet he said something to them which leads to the second principle of Servant Leaders versus Lording Leaders.

He said, "I have set you an example that you should do as I have done for you." JOHN 13:15

The second principle is:

Principle #2: Servant Leaders develop others. Lording Leaders dictate over others.

Notice what Jesus did. He was modeling something for them, but He was doing it for a reason. He was doing it to help develop them, so they could become the same type of leader that He was.

For years, when reading books on leadership, a good delegating leader was almost the epitome of the highest level of leadership. They taught leaders to delegate away whatever you can to others. "Look at that great leader and the way they delegate," they said.

However, we've come to realize that delegation is sometimes just a nicer word for a dictator. The truth is, there is an even better level of leadership than delegating and it is developing.

When you develop someone else, you are investing in them and their leadership. You're not treating them like a pawn on your chess board but instead you're setting them up to play their own game of chess.

Servant Leaders recognize their greatest job is developing others for success. Lording Leaders see people as pawns that they use for their own personal success.

Many leadership books have taught the simple process of developing others through the following model:

- I do, you watch, we talk.
- I do, you help, we talk.
- You do, I help, we talk.
- You do, I watch, we talk.
- You do!

The reality is if you follow the life of Christ with His disciples you can see where He took His disciples through this very process to develop them. Jesus was about leadership development way before it was cool or trendy. It's what a good Servant Leader does. Their heart is to see the success of the other individual and develop them toward that end. It is the greatest calling of a leader's life.

I'm so grateful for the role that Dennis Pierce played in the life of my wife years ago. Dennis was the Worship Pastor at a church I worked for in Minnesota. For years my wife sang on Dennis's teams and also volunteered to oversee worship for our kids' mid-week ministry. During those years,

Dennis saw something in Lisa. He saw leadership in her, he saw potential and possibilities in her. He saw her as one worth developing in the realm of worship leading. So one Sunday he asked if she would lead worship for the weekend. He would help her, he would be on the team, but she would lead. That day something ignited in Lisa that had never been there before. Perhaps it was a vision of what she was capable of or just a taste of something God had designed her to do, and once she tasted it, she knew it was what she was made for. That was just the first time she led worship. Dennis graciously provided more opportunities for her to lead during our weekend services and as they say, the rest is history. Lisa has been the Worship Pastor at Lakeland for years now and no one would deny this is what she is wired to do. But it all started with Dennis who was willing to develop another leader to do exactly what he was doing. Dennis is still leading worship in churches. But now, so is Lisa.

DAILY DISCOVERY/ SKEPTIC'S CHALLENGE: Do you have a tendency to dictate or delegate to others? Who helped you develop in life? Let's take a big step today into developing someone else. Your first step is to identify who that potential leader might be. Some of the most powerful conversations are when someone says to another, "I see in you" the ability to be, or the opportunity for you to become, etc. Who can you see as a future leader? How can you start the process of developing them today?

NOTES

WEEK TEN / DAY THREE

SERVANT LEADER VS. LORDING LEADER: LETTING OPPORTUNITIES ARISE

26 "But among you it will be different. Those who are the greatest among you should take the lowest rank, and the leader should be like a servant. 27 Who is more important, the one who sits at the table or the one who serves? The one who sits at the table, of course. But not here! For I am among you as one who serves."

LUKE 22:26-27 (NLT)

Have you ever known someone to just walk into a room or into a problem that a team is trying to solve and take over? They take the baton of leadership out of whoever's hand it is in and in a domineering way, take charge.

I've seen it, because I've been that person at times. It's not a pretty scene. In fact, I have to be really conscious of my actions when I walk into a space because I can easily slide into that role as a Lording Leader.

Jesus modeled something different as a Servant Leader. In the book of Luke, Jesus is with His disciples and an argument breaks out among them about who will be the greatest. Let's check it out in Luke 22.

24 "Then they began to argue among themselves about who would be the greatest among them. 25 Jesus told them, 'In this world the kings and great men lord it over their people, yet they are called 'friends of the people.' 26 But among you it will be different. Those who are the greatest among you should take the lowest rank, and the leader should be like a servant. 27 Who is more important, the one who sits at the table or the one who serves? The one who sits at the table, of course. But not here! For I am among you as one who serves.

28 'You have stayed with me in my time of trial. 29 And just as my Father has granted me a Kingdom, I now grant you the right 30 to eat and drink at my table in my Kingdom. And you will sit on thrones, judging the twelve tribes of Israel.'" LUKE 22:24-30 (NLT)

Jesus and the disciples lived in an era when lording your position, power, and leadership over others was common practice. Hence this is not the only conversation Jesus had with His disciples in response to their arguments about who was the greatest among them. Verse 30 is pretty eye opening and insightful to the principles of servant leadership. Jesus actually gives the disciples a glimpse into the reward they will receive for their servant leadership. He says, "You will sit on thrones beside me in the kingdom of heaven." Basically, Jesus is saying, "If you lead with servant hearts and serve with all you are, you'll be raised to a level of leadership and honor that will astound you."

But the key here is to lead as a Servant Leader. Serve others first. Don't chase after leadership, influence, and power. If you lead as a Servant Leader, leadership, influence, and power will all come to you in God's perfect timing.

We don't have to run after leading. We run after serving and leadership will come.

The third principle of Servant Leaders vs. Lording Leaders is:

Principle #3: Servant Leaders allow leadership opportunities to arise. Lording Leaders fight to lead.

One of the guys who modeled this better than anyone else I've ever known is Gary Witt. When Gary came to our church, he carried with him quite a resume both in the marketplace and volunteer positions at past churches. He had a degree from Harvard, multiple high-level roles in corporations, and a current role as president over a major branch of a multi-billion dollar corporation and largest employer in our county. In churches he had always found himself sitting on church boards and helping make major decisions in the life and direction of the church.

The first time I met Gary, I could see all his leadership potential and natural ability to serve in the church. But in that first meeting he said to me, "Josh, I lead in almost everything I've done in life, for the first year we are here at the church, you let me know how I can serve and I'll do it. If you want me to hold babies in the nursery, I'll do it. If you want me to open doors and greet people, I'll do it. If you want me to be an usher, I'll do it. If you want me to scrub the toilets and clean the bathrooms between services, I'll do it. Just let me serve for a year in whatever capacity you need."

That's exactly what Gary did. I'm pretty sure he did all of the above: held babies, opened doors, and ushered; maybe the only exception was scrubbing toilets. But he humbly served until I couldn't wait any longer and begged him to join our Business Operations Team. And he's been serving in leadership roles at the church ever since. But he proved he was the right type of leader (a Servant Leader) to serve at the church by not fighting to lead, but instead allowing leadership opportunities to come to him.

If you're chasing after influence and leadership, you're following a worldly model that will likely turn you into a Lording Leader. Perhaps we can be people who aim to serve first and allow leadership opportunities to arise. These are the leaders people truly want to follow. Not those who are hungry for power and leadership, but those who are hungry to serve.

DAILY DISCOVERY/ SKEPTIC'S CHALLENGE: Where have you been chasing after influence and leadership? Is it possible that if you stop chasing and start serving, God might present an opportunity in His perfect timing? If there is an area where you desire to lead, take a first step toward simply serving in that place. Allow God to raise you to leadership. You'll be the best leader (a Servant Leader) when the time comes for you to lead.

WEEK TEN / DAY FOUR

SERVANT LEADER VS. LORDING LEADER: MOTIVATING WITH LOVE, GRACE, AND ENCOURAGEMENT

"just as the Son of Man did not come to be served, but to serve, and to give his life as a ransom for many."

MATTHEW 20:28 (NASB)

Jesus, who models Servant Leadership, motivates us to follow His model through the greatest display of love that has ever been shown. This was displayed at the cross.

One of my favorite TV shows over the years has been *Survivor*. I love the physical challenge it poses, I love the team and relational dynamics, and I love the competitive nature of it. Over the years some individuals from the show have become known as villains and others as heroes. There are even seasons where the cast is made up of all former villains vs. heroes. What gets an individual dubbed as a villain versus a hero is summarized in this fourth principle.

Principle #4: Servant Leaders motivate by love, grace, and encouragement. Lording Leaders motivate by fear, guilt, or shame.

The villains are always Lording Leaders who motivate the other competitors through fear, guilt, and shame. In the end, the other competitors bend to the villain's leadership demands, but usually hate them for it and lose all respect for the villain along the way. The heroes become heroes because they step into places of leadership for the team, but they do so through the display of love, grace, and encouragement.

We see Jesus lead one of his closest disciples back into his role as a leader, but with such grace and love. The disciple is Peter. On the night of Christ's arrest, Peter is confronted three times about his association with

Jesus. On all three occasions, Peter, who is one of Jesus' closest friends and followers, denies that he even knows Jesus.

After such a painful betrayal, how does Jesus restore that relationship? How will He lead Peter back to his former level of commitment and even exceed it? We find the account in John 21:15-17.

15 "When they had finished eating, Jesus said to Simon Peter, 'Simon son of John, do you love me more than these?'
'Yes, LORD,' he said, 'you know that I love you.'
Jesus said, 'Feed my lambs.'
16 Again Jesus said, 'Simon son of John, do you love me?'
He answered, 'Yes, LORD, you know that I love you.'
Jesus said, 'Take care of my sheep.'
17 The third time he said to him, 'Simon son of John, do you love me?'
Peter was hurt because Jesus asked him the third time, 'Do you love me?'
He said, 'LORD, you know all things; you know that I love you.'
Jesus said, 'Feed my sheep.'" JOHN 21:15-17

After Peter had denied Jesus three times, it's like Jesus takes Peter on a little restoration journey. Three times he denied Jesus, now three times Jesus will ask, "Do you love me?" What he's asking is, are you really with me? When Peter says yes, notice Jesus' response each time: "Then I commission you again to your calling," "Feed my sheep," "Take care of my sheep," "Feed my sheep."

Jesus reinstates Peter with love and grace.

Another leadership principle is that what we lead "with" we duplicate. Meaning, unhealthy leaders produce unhealthy followers who will become unhealthy future leaders. Those who were led by fear, guilt, and shame will lead others with fear, guilt, and shame.

What Jesus does here is He leads Peter back into his calling with love, grace, patience, and encouragement.

Maybe you learned how to lead with fear, guilt, and shame from a parent, sibling, boss, or even a close friend. No matter where you picked it up, if that is how you motivate people to follow, you've picked up an unhealthy approach of Lording Leadership. In the end, you're more likely to be viewed as a villain than the Servant Leader who motivates with love, grace, and encouragement and truly is a hero to those they lead.

DAILY DISCOVERY/ SKEPTIC'S CHALLENGE: When you lead are you more likely to lead through fear, guilt, and shame or love, grace, and encouragement? Today let's take a step toward our hero (Jesus) and His leadership style by motivating others through love, grace, and encouragement. Let's aim to be the most loving, grace-filled, and encouraging leaders our followers have ever known.

NOTES

WEEK TEN / DAY FIVE

SERVANT LEADER VS. LORDING LEADER: FOCUSING ON THE SUCCESS OF THE NEXT GENERATION

19 "Therefore go and make disciples of all nations, baptizing them in the name of the Father and of the Son and of the Holy Spirit, 20 and teaching them to obey everything I have commanded you. And surely I am with you always, to the very end of the age."

MATTHEW 28:19-20

When Jesus gives this commissioning to his disciples, He is handing out no small task. Go and make disciples everywhere, in every nation—oh, and p.s., this is going to take a while. You're going to have to make disciples who make disciples who make disciples who make disciples. It will take until the end of the age. Meaning, you're always going to have to keep your eyes focused on the next generation.

This leads us to the fifth principle of Servant Leaders vs. Lording Leaders:

Principle #5: Servant Leaders focus on the success of the next generation. Lording Leaders focus on their current success.

In scripture we have plenty of examples to choose from but I want to highlight two.

The first is Moses. Moses has been told that he won't lead the Israelites into the promised land. Notice his concern found in the book of Numbers.

15 "Moses said to the LORD, 16 'May the LORD, the God who gives breath to all living things, appoint someone over this community 17 to go out and come in before them, one who will lead them out and bring them in, so the LORD's people will not be like sheep without a shepherd.'"

NUMBERS 27:15-17

His concern is centered around what will happen after him. He is concerned for the nation and the generations to come. So he uses his leadership to set up the next generation for success. He will raise up Joshua to care for and lead the nation and the coming generations.

Conversely, check out another leader over Israel during another era.

Hezekiah is the king. Near the end of his life he gloats of his great wealth by showing it off to the king of Babylon. Because of this the LORD sends Isaiah with a message to Hezekiah in 2 Kings 20:17-19.

17 "The time is coming when everything in your palace—all the treasures stored up by your ancestors until now—will be carried off to Babylon. Nothing will be left, says the LORD. 18 Some of your very own sons will be taken away into exile. They will become eunuchs who will serve in the palace of Babylon's king."
19 Then Hezekiak said to Isaiah, 'This message you have given me from the LORD is good.' For the king was thinking, 'At least there will be peace and security during my lifetime.'" 2 KINGS 20:17-19 (NLT)

While Hezekiah has just received some shocking news, what's more shocking is his response. The news is his wealth is going to be carried away to Babylon and even some of his kids are going to be carried away to Babylon. But instead of sorrow or brokenness his response is, "It's all good, at least I won't experience it in my lifetime." He has a very short-sighted view of his leadership and his kingdom.

A good leader, a Servant Leader, is looking for ways to set up the next generation for success. Sometimes we think about this through the lens of legacy. Some companies close their doors when the founder retires simply because no one was ever developed to take the spot of the founding leader. Their legacy is snuffed out before it ever began. Short-sighted leaders are focused on their personal success. However, long-lasting legacy is seen only years later when the harder and sometimes slower work of developing the next generation is complete. Servant Leaders lead toward that end. They desire to lead the next generation toward success, and by default, they create a lasting legacy for themselves.

DAILY DISCOVERY/ SKEPTIC'S CHALLENGE: We all lead someone. We all can influence others to some degree. The question is whether your influence and leadership will carry the traits of a Servant Leader or a Lording Leader. Today, let's dream for a bit about the next generation. Take five minutes to dream about an impact you could make that could become a true legacy. What or who can you invest in today that will outlast you and set up the future generation for success?

NOTES

WEEK TEN / DAY SIX & SEVEN

DAY 6: LET THAT THOUGHT SIMMER

What idea was most challenging to you this week?

DAY 7: LET THAT THOUGHT SIMMER

What day from this week or concept do you want to rethink about?

NOTES

WEEK ELEVEN

WEEK ELEVEN / DAY ONE

VICTOR VS. VICTIM: REMINDING OR QUESTIONING

4 "For every child of God defeats this evil world, and we achieve this victory through our faith. 5 And who can win this battle against the world? Only those who believe that Jesus is the Son of God."

1 JOHN 5:4-5 (NLT)

In my first job as a student pastor I had a young adult leader who could never take responsibility for his part in anything that ever went wrong. If he was supposed to be overseeing the gym and he wasn't there, and an issue took place because no adult was present, he would deflect his responsibility and make an excuse. Or I might walk outside and he would be standing on top of the church bus with some students. As I would confront him about that foolish decision, he would make an excuse and deflect any responsibility.

Do you know anyone like that? Someone who struggles to apologize, someone who always has an excuse? Perhaps that person is you. Take an honest assessment of yourself. When something goes wrong, what is your immediate response? Do you make an excuse or take responsibility?

MAIN IDEA: A Victor vs. Victim mindset reveals the heart around taking responsibility and our posture toward excuses. A Victim denies responsibility and makes excuses, a Victor takes responsibility and overcomes excuses.

Perhaps you've unintentionally picked up an identity or thought process that reflects a Victim mindset. If you're a Christ follower, this is an identity that is no longer yours. If you don't claim to be a Christian, this week will offer insights to mindsets as a Victor that God desires for humanity. Will you be willing to explore those mindsets and take an honest look at the perspective you currently carry?

There are four contrasting mindsets of a Victor vs. Victim. The first one is:

Principle #1: Victors remind themselves of who God is. Victims question who God is.

One of Jesus' relatives is John the Baptist. John is like a wild prophet who spent most of his time out in the wilderness calling Jews to repentance and obedience to God. He is also known as the forerunner to Christ's ministry. Meaning, before Jesus started teaching, performing miracles, or gathering any disciples, John had already been doing that for years. In many ways his ministry prepared people's hearts for Jesus' ministry. Along the way, John made some enemies. One powerful enemy was Herod Antipas. John had publicly rebuked Herod for divorcing his wife and taking his brother's wife to be his own. This public rebuke landed John in jail. It's from this place that John sent a message to Jesus.

2 "When John, who was in prison, heard about the deeds of the Messiah, he sent his disciples 3 to ask him, 'Are you the one who is to come, or should we expect someone else?'" MATTHEW 11:2-3

John found himself questioning Jesus' identity. Maybe he's also simply questioning Jesus' goodness? Jesus' ability to save?

The reason why he questions Jesus may be because he's hearing all the amazing miracles that are taking place out THERE, but John needs a miracle right HERE (in prison). And because of his situation, he is questioning Jesus' identity.

This is so fascinating, because this is John. He is a relative and friend of Jesus. But most importantly, he was the first person who publicly declared the identity of Jesus as the Messiah. He is probably the most sold-out for Christ. Yet his position in prison has him questioning everything.

He feels like a victim and he's questioning if Jesus is the Savior, or if we should look for someone else.

I don't want you to think you can never question God, but here's the point:

Don't question where God has already brought you clarity.

Another way to say it would be, there is no need to raise a question where God has already brought you an answer.

For example, if God impresses on your heart how much He loves you, don't be surprised when the devil attacks that specific promise or reality. Remember the devil loves to steal, kill and destroy. So of course he would want to steal the promises that have been impressed on your heart. What we must do is remind ourselves of the truth that God brought to us with clarity.

For John already had great clarity around the answer for the question he raised. We see that clarity in John 1.

"The next day John saw Jesus coming toward him and said, 'Look, the Lamb of God, who takes away the sin of the world!" JOHN 1:29

So John has already had one of the most profound and clear revelations of the identity of Jesus, but his pain accentuates his victimization.

A Victor mindset must remind themselves who God is, while a victim will start to question the character traits of God that God has clearly impressed upon them in the past.

DAILY DISCOVERY: What are one or two things that God has clearly impressed on your heart? (Perhaps it's something He impressed upon you while going through this book.) Have you felt like those things were attacked directly, meaning you've found yourself wondering if they are true? This is not surprising because the enemy always wants to steal the very truths that have been promised to you. Today let's declare those truths over our hearts just like the day we received them. This is the Victor mindset, reminding our hearts what is ours and what is true.

SKEPTIC'S CHALLENGE/ PRAYER: When I ask most people who claim they don't believe in God to consider this question they usually have an answer. If God did exist, was there ever a time in your life when you would say, "God was close to me here" or you could fill in the blank of "I have seen God _____." Most can fill in that blank. How would you fill it in? Now, can we give God the benefit of the doubt for a moment and answer, "If God was showing you something about Himself, what was He showing you?" Try out faith for a bit, by reminding yourself what He was revealing to you about Himself in that moment.

NOTES

WEEK ELEVEN / DAY TWO

VICTOR VS. VICTIM:
THE TEAM IS WINNING OR I AM LOSING

4 "Jesus replied, 'Go back and report to John what you hear and see: 5 The blind receive sight, the lame walk, those who have leprosy are cleansed, the deaf hear, the dead are raised, and the good news is proclaimed to the poor."

MATTHEW 11:4-5

I love paintball. Not that I get to play too often, but when I do get to play it's always exhilarating. I think it's the combination of competition, the feeling of a battle or war, the reality that there is real pain involved when you get shot (but no one is dying) and team strategies.

Sometimes the strategies are perfect for a game setting, although not accurate to how anyone would fight a real battle if life and death were in the balance. For example, I've played rounds where the strategy is that I am the decoy to draw all the firepower in my direction, knowing I would get eliminated, but setting my team up for the win.

There are situations we will face in life where we feel like something is a complete loss, but God in His sovereignty sees how it fits into the bigger picture and IS PRODUCING A WIN for the kingdom (for the team).

The second principle of a Victor vs. Victim mindset is:

Principle #2: Victors focus on the team win. Victims focus on their personal losses.

Picking up our story from yesterday with John the Baptist in prison, this is what John is doing. He is focused on his current circumstance and is seeing it as a loss. But notice what Jesus says to him about what he needs to focus on.

4 "Jesus replied, 'Go back and report to John what you hear and see: 5 The blind receive sight, the lame walk, those who have leprosy are cleansed, the deaf hear, the dead are raised, and the good news is proclaimed to the poor." MATTHEW 11:4-5

John is fixated on HIS situation. His situation is bad. His life is being threatened. His ministry is stalled out. He's alone, and he doesn't like it.

He is focusing on his personal state of loss. But notice Jesus' response to him. To tell John this, "Tell him all the good you see and hear is happening."

Victims have a tendency to focus their attention on themselves and their struggles, while Victors focus their attention on what God is doing and where He is overcoming struggles. Victors remind themselves of where the team is winning even in the midst of their personal struggles.

I'm not going to lie. Sometimes life just gets hard and it's difficult to not let our mind center around the pain we feel or the hurdle we are facing. Yet this is exactly what Jesus is challenging John to do. Spend your time rehearsing (or focusing on) where God is working, where the Kingdom is winning, and where the team is taking ground.

In some small ways maybe this process is simply about reminding ourselves that this life we live is not an individual sport, it's a team sport. You're still on the winning team even if in your situation you feel like you're currently losing. You are still a part of the victorious team, so you can carry the mindset of a Victor.

"And we know that in all things God works for the good of those who love him, who have been called according to his purpose." ROMANS 8:28

Romans reminds us that God is working all things, including the times like John where you feel like you're just stuck in prison, for good. It's all a part of the victory God is producing within the team. Thus, our mindset can be that of a Victor.

At every staff meeting, we begin by sharing "wins." This is an opportunity to share where God is working and winning in individual ministries or in the church as a whole. We do this for the very principle discussed here. There are weeks when staff members might feel like they've just "lost" at every turn. But taking the time to remind our hearts where God is winning and that we are a part of the winning team, anchors our hearts in our victorious identity.

How about you? Are you spinning your wheels, fixated on your own personal loss? Or are you taking ground by focusing on the team's wins?

DAILY DISCOVERY: List two to three situations where God is winning. Now thank God for those wins, celebrate His goodness that is seen in those situations. Take some time to turn over your own personal struggles to God and trust Him with them. Then remind your heart of the victory that you are a part of and the identity as a Victor that you carry.

SKEPTIC'S CHALLENGE/ PRAYER: Do you have a tendency to fester in a Victim mindset focusing on your personal pain? Have you ever seen someone's struggle turned around and used for someone else's good? Could you give God the benefit of the doubt and consider how He might use the pain of your past for some overall good in your life or in someone else's life?

NOTES

WEEK ELEVEN / DAY THREE

VICTOR VS. VICTIM: THANKSGIVING OR OFFENSE

"Blessed is anyone who does not stumble [or is not offended] on account of me."

MATTHEW 11:6

A spirit of offense is pretty easy to pick up. None of us like it when life hits the fan, a family member dies, a sickness invades your life, your finances are in crisis, your marriage is on the rocks, or when your addiction continually rears its ugly head, and we look for someone to blame. We pick up this spirit of offense toward God. It is usually centered around the question, "Why did God allow this?"

We are offended that God allowed this or that to happen.

Back to John the Baptist in prison. He's questioning if Jesus is the Savior he thought Jesus would be. He knows Jesus is saving other people's lives left and right, and he's offended that Jesus hasn't come and saved his life yet.

When Jesus responds to him in Matthew 11:6, he begins by saying "Blessed…" Blessed can literally be translated as happy. Meaning, "John, you can be happy in prison right now if you choose to not be offended by me."

If I were to ask what is the opposite of offense, I think it might be thanksgiving.

6 "Do not be anxious about anything, but in every situation, by prayer and petition, with thanksgiving, present your requests to God. 7 And the peace of God, which transcends all understanding, will guard your hearts and your minds in Christ Jesus." PHILIPPIANS 4:6-7

I believe the qualifier of our attitudes described in Philippians is key. It's not like the verses say, "Hey, when life is anxious and difficult, just pray about it and God will give you peace." No, he says, present those prayers and petitions to God, with thanksgiving. Meaning our attitude as we present those prayers matters. There are few things that will break the grip of the enemy and power He is trying to exert in your life more than thanksgiving.

Proverbs 17:22 says, "A thankful heart is good medicine."

Thanksgiving is like medicine that brings healing to the sickness of offense.

This leads to the third principle of a Victor vs. Victim mindset:

Principle #3: Victors have a spirit of thanksgiving. Victims have a spirit of offense.

What's also interesting is how Jesus responds to John. He actually quotes a well-known prophetic passage from the book of Isaiah that Jews believed would be an indicator of the work of the Messiah.

5 "Then will the eyes of the blind be opened
    and the ears of the deaf unstopped.
6 Then will the lame leap like a deer,
    and the mute tongue shout for joy..." ISAIAH 35:5-6

But there is one more line from the passage in Isaiah that Jesus leaves off. Jesus leaves off the part of the passage where it says, "and prisoners will be freed." ISAIAH 61:1 (NLT)

Jesus is ultimately saying, "Yes, I am the Messiah, I am fulfilling all the prophecies of the Messiah. However, John, in your case, the answer is no. You're not going to get out of prison. But it doesn't change the fact that I am who you believed Me to be. And you can be happy right where you're at if you don't let the spirit of offense rob you of what God can do with you. You can endure with a joyful spirit if you grab hold of a spirit of thanksgiving around the team win."

DAILY DISCOVERY: Today we are going to try to be the most thankful people on the planet. If thanksgiving has the ability to break the power and strongholds of the enemy, then we want to give thanks over everything today. To solidify a Victor's identity, we carry thanksgiving everywhere we go.

SKEPTIC'S CHALLENGE/ PRAYER: Do you find yourself offended by ways in which God has worked or maybe appeared not to work in your life? If you foster offense you'll find yourself slipping into the identity of a victim. Consider how you can try on a thankful heart for a change. If a thankful heart is good medicine, give thanks all throughout the day and see if it seems to bring a sense of healing to your heart.

NOTES

WEEK ELEVEN / DAY FOUR

VICTOR VS. VICTIM: ENFORCING THE WIN OR APATHETICALLY WAITING

"They triumphed over him
  by the blood of the Lamb
  and by the word of their testimony..."

REVELATION 12:11

Years ago I remember driving through town and seeing a woman out walking her dog. The funny thing is I don't know who was really walking who. It is one of the most hilarious images that will forever be in my mind. This woman was holding on for dear life, with one hand on the leash and the other flying frantically behind her. Her legs barely stayed beneath her as she was pulled sideways at a speed that she clearly could not keep up with. Her face was filled with terror and exhaustion. And of course, I just laughed. I guess the "godly" thing to do would have probably been to jump out of my car and save her, but I was just laughing too hard.

She didn't know how to enforce the fact that she was in charge, and the dog was clearly taking advantage of the situation.

The truth is, there are plenty of Christians going through life hanging on for dear life just like that woman. They look terrified and exhausted and the devil is having a hay day with them. They haven't figured out how to enforce the fact that they are in charge and that they are the victors. Instead, they live like victims being dragged through life with identities as victims.

The fourth principle of the Victor vs. Victim mindset is:

Principle #4: Victors know they enforce the win. Victims do nothing, waiting for God to bring the win.

In Revelation we see an amazing picture of the victory that followers of Christ have. In the context of chapter 12, God gives us a glimpse into Satan's original fall from heaven. He is cast out of heaven and hurled down to dwell on earth until his final judgment. We see the interactions of Christ followers with him until that day.

10 "Then I heard a loud voice in heaven say:
'Now have come the salvation and the power
  and the kingdom of our God,
  and the authority of his Messiah.
For the accuser of our brothers and sisters,
  who accuses them before our God day and night,
  has been hurled down.
11 They triumphed over him
  by the blood of the Lamb
  and by the word of their testimony;
they did not love their lives so much
  as to shrink from death." REVELATION 12:10-11

Let me make a few quick observations. First, "They" in verse 11 are Christians. And they have triumphed over him, Satan. One of the greatest lies the devil tells us is that only Jesus, or strong—really strong—angels, or perhaps super-spiritual people, can overcome the devil and the works of the devil. But that's just not true. They, being Christians, every single one of them triumphs over the devil. We are triumphant not because of anything we can DO but because of what Jesus DID. It says, *"They triumphed over him by the blood of the Lamb."* Meaning, it is Christ's death that gave us our victory, but it is for all of us who put our trust in Jesus, not just the select few or the super-spiritual ones.

So what is Satan doing to keep us from enforcing that victory? He's doing the only thing he can do. He's accusing us. The verse says, *"For the accuser of our brothers and sisters, who accuses them before our God day and night."* This is all that Satan has left: a lie of accusation is what the devil is scrambling to hold onto.

The devil keeps accusing because he knows he's losing.

He's accusing us day and night, trying to get us to buy any lie he is selling so that we won't step into our identities as Victors over him and enforce that victory that we have through Christ.

For example, if you've ever struggled with an addiction, one of the lies the enemy perpetuates is that you will never be free from this addiction. No matter what you do, you will always struggle with it and always fall to it again. The reality is, all the devil has left is that accusation. And the devil's work survives on lies.

It's crazy that God, in His bizarre plan, sees fit by the work of the cross and the power of the Holy Spirit within lowly humanity, to use us to enforce the victory over one of the strongest fallen angels to ever exist.

1 John 4:4 says "...greater is He [Christ and the work of the cross] who is in you, than he [Satan] who is in the world." (NASB)

In this principle, that Victims do nothing, waiting for God to bring the win. It's not that Victims necessarily deny that Christ won a victory at the cross, they simply don't see themselves as carriers or enforcers of that victory. As a result, they get caught in the doom and gloom reports around the world. They sometimes take a "hunker-down" approach to life. They hide within their church walls or their small groups, just wanting to make it through this life into eternity. They see every place where the devil is working and they unintentionally diminish the power of the cross by being wowed by the power of the devil.

In fact, fear is an indicator of any time we've allowed ourselves to become impressed by the work of the devil over the work of Christ.

The Victim has forgotten, or has never been told, that they are the ones that enforce the victory over the devil. They are meant to carry the identity of a Victor into a dark and broken world.

In rugby there is something that is called a scrum. A scrum is when the two teams line up head to head and go into what looks like a two-team deadlock. From the top it kind of looks like a spider with legs spreading out from the two teams in opposite directions. It usually appears like neither team is pushing the other in either direction while they are scrambling to pass the ball between their legs and get it out to one of their team members to run it. Sometimes the scrum will start to move in one direction as one team gets a better footing. And once the scrum starts moving it's inevitable that the team with the momentum just pushes the other one back.

The devil would love to get you to think that you're caught in a deadlock. But sometimes you need to remind the devil that you've got all the momentum because of the work of the cross. The work of Christ and the Holy Spirit is going to drive him back, and your identity is in Christ as a victor.

DAILY DISCOVERY: If Christ's victory over the enemy is my victory over the enemy, where have I been allowing the enemy to pull me around in life, like the woman being walked by her dog? With a Victor's mindset, what truth do I need to declare over my life today?

SKEPTIC'S CHALLENGE/ PRAYER: I don't know if you believe that the devil exists. But if you would consider that his primary attack upon humanity is in the form of accusing us and lying, what lie might you be believing that is keeping you living as a Victim? What victory do you think God would desire for you?

NOTES

WEEK ELEVEN / DAY FIVE

THE HIDDEN LANDMINES OF IDENTITY: ISOLATION

9 "Two are better than one,
   because they have a good return for their labor:
10 If either of them falls down,
   one can help the other up.
But pity anyone who falls
   and has no one to help them up.
11 Also, if two lie down together, they will keep warm.
   But how can one keep warm alone?
12 Though one may be overpowered,
   two can defend themselves..."

ECCLESIASTES 4:9-12

You've probably heard or seen stories of celebrities who have had major downfalls in their careers. Sometimes it's due to substance abuse or a mental crisis, a scandal, or embezzlement, or a lie or an accusation. But any way you look at it, it takes them out. They go from fame and fortune to a failure and flop overnight. Often at the crux of their fall is a hidden mine in the foundation of their identity. When these hidden landmines are stumbled upon, they often trigger a crisis of identity.

To help us avoid a potential downfall or explosion in our identities, there are common landmines that we can look for in our lives. To explore these hidden mines of identity we are going to return to King David.

During week 5, we looked at King David as one who established a healthy inner image. The way he viewed God and the way he viewed himself set him up to be a giant slayer. And while David's story began with such promise, he didn't make it through life unscathed by his own mistakes. No, David actually had quite a mid-life crisis downfall. And within his downfall we can see a handful of buried mines in his identity which remained ignored and resulted in a pretty painful crash.

If we can head into our final week with a sense of humility and caution, we will likely be able to dig up some potential mines in each of our lives that, if addressed, can save us from a major fall.

The first buried landmine of identity is:

Landmine #1: Isolation and a lack of accountability.

Let's hop right into the middle of David's story. David spends years under the poor leadership of King Saul till Saul's life comes to its bitter end in a battle. When David is made king he leads Israel to become a well established, strong and honored nation. He is loved by his people, he is loved by his army, and he genuinely loves God and is loved by God. He has everything going in the right direction for him and his kingdom, until 2 Samuel 11. This is what it says.

"In the spring, at the time when kings go off to war, David sent Joab out with the king's men and the whole Israelite army. They destroyed the Ammonites and besieged Rabbah. But David remained in Jerusalem."
2 SAMUEL 11:1

Do you see it? *"At the time when kings go off to war... David remained in Jerusalem."*

Where should David be? As the king, he should be where all the kings are. Off at war, with their men, leading the charge. But instead, David is at home, alone. He is in the wrong place, at the wrong time, with no accountability.

Have you found yourself in isolation from healthy relationships? Sure there is some freedom there, but there is also no accountability there. There is no one close enough to call you out on your "stuff."

In Ecclesiastes 4:12 it says, "Though one may be overpowered, two can defend themselves..."

The temptations that present themselves when you're living in isolation often feel overwhelming. Ecclesiastes describes the situation as a place where you can be overpowered. However, when someone is close beside you and temptation comes, you'll be able to defend yourself from it.

The whole point is that there is an advantage in making sure you're not doing life alone.

I've said it many times. Isolation is the devil's playground. It's because we don't have someone to check our thoughts with. We don't have someone to keep us from stumbling. The devil is a liar and it's easy to fester alone in a lie.

Let's keep our eyes open for this landmine to our identity!

DAILY DISCOVERY/ SKEPTIC'S CHALLENGE: Simply ask yourself, who in your life can ask you the hard questions? Does anyone have a voice to challenge you, to call you up, or call you out? Who could you reach out to today to invite them into a closer relationship with you for the purpose of calling each other up and calling each other out?

NOTES

WEEK ELEVEN / DAY SIX & SEVEN

DAY 6: LET THAT THOUGHT SIMMER

What idea was most challenging to you this week?

DAY 7: LET THAT THOUGHT SIMMER

What day from this week or concept do you want to rethink about?

NOTES

WEEK TWELVE

WEEK TWELVE / DAY ONE

THE HIDDEN LANDMINES OF IDENTITY: PRIDE AND POWER

"Pride goes before destruction,
  a haughty spirit before a fall."

PROVERBS 16:18

The story of Bonnie and Clyde may be one of the most famous endings to any crime couple in history. It's about a young couple who fall in love and travel the country with their gang during the Great Depression. They are known for their bank robberies and felonies. Their exploits captured the attention of the American press which sometimes glamorized their crimes. Their demise is what they are most known for, as their car and bodies were riddled with bullets from police in an ambush that ended their lives. They were a couple so full of their own pride and power they just couldn't see how it was leading them to their fall.

Like you, I've heard way too many stories of powerful people falling into major moral failures. Whether former presidents, pastors, movie or music stars, millionaires, or some other realm of significant influence and power, their falls all are similar. They came to a place, just like Bonnie and Clyde, where they felt untouchable.

This is the second hidden landmine to our identities:

Landmine #2: Pride and Power

We are back in 2 Samuel looking at the life of King David. Remember, it was the time of year when the kings went off to war—but David stayed home. He's already in a dangerous place of isolation, but now he will trip on this second hidden mine.

2 "One evening David got up from his bed and walked around on the roof of the palace. From the roof he saw a woman bathing. The woman was very beautiful,

3 and David sent someone to find out about her. The man said, "She is Bathsheba, the daughter of Eliam and the wife of Uriah the Hittite."

4 Then David sent messengers to get her. She came to him, and he slept with her. (Now she was purifying herself from her monthly uncleanness.) Then she went back home." 2 SAMUEL 11:2-4

In verse 3, David's servant gives Bathsheba a family context. Up until this point, David maybe could have believed she was just a woman living in his kingdom. But now he's being made aware that she's not just any woman; she's a daughter, she's a wife. Think about the father and how he would feel about his daughter being placed in this inappropriate situation. Think about the husband and how he would feel about his wife being placed in this situation. Think about Bathsheba—perhaps she desires to do what's right, but feels like she has no choice. I doubt David considers any of these individuals.

I wonder if David thinks he's untouchable. I would argue at this point in his life he is drunk in his own pride and power and has lost sight of others' feelings. And an affair that should have never happened begins.

Pride and power can set one up to do the most foolish things because we're so indulged in self and our sense of personal control.

Proverbs tells us that pride goes before destruction, a haughty spirit before a fall.

The book of Proverbs is like billboards along the side of the highway of our life. If God could put up billboards to get our attention, send us messages, and give us warnings, this one is as blatant as it can be. Pride comes before the fall. So beware of pride in your life. Beware of power and how it can make you blind to destructive beliefs and behaviors.

This billboard message turned out to be true in David's life. Let's keep our eyes open for this hidden mine before it becomes true in ours.

DAILY DISCOVERY/ SKEPTIC'S CHALLENGE: Let me propose some questions that can help us open our eyes to this potential hidden mine in our lives. Do you usually have control and like having control in your life? Would anyone call you a control freak? Do you control situations or people through influence, leadership, position, or money? Have your words or actions wounded anyone recently? Could you see in advance that your words or actions would have that impact, or were you blind to others' feelings? Take an honest assessment of your own personal pride and power. Ask God to help you to stay humble in these areas.

NOTES

WEEK TWELVE / DAY TWO

THE HIDDEN LANDMINES OF IDENTITY: WHEN CHARACTER COMES UP SHORT

"Whoever walks in integrity walks securely,
but whoever takes crooked paths will be found out."
PROVERBS 10:9

"May integrity and uprightness protect me,
because my hope, LORD, is in you."
PSALM 25:21

Do you know what these people have in common: Erin Moran, Gary Coleman, Dana Plato, Miley Cyrus, Lindsay Lohan, Justin Bieber? They all had pretty major crashes as child pop stars. While some recovered and re-entered the limelight, others never did. My argument specifically around child pop stars is that they simply don't have the character traits or maturity to handle the weight of their fame, influence, and fortune.

The third hidden landmine of identity is:

Landmine #3: When character doesn't measure up to your leadership, influence, or level of success.

Let's hop back into the account of King David with Bathsheba. David has just slept with another man's wife and the result of that is a pregnancy. What is he going to do now? Let's pick it up in 2 Samuel 11.

5 "The woman conceived and sent word to David, saying, 'I am pregnant.' 6 So David sent this word to Joab [the commander of the army]: 'Send me Uriah the Hittite.' And Joab sent him to David. 7 When Uriah came to him, David asked him how Joab was, how the soldiers were and how the war was going. 8 Then David said to Uriah, 'Go down to your house and wash your feet.' So Uriah left the palace, and a gift from the king was

sent after him. 9 But Uriah slept at the entrance to the palace with all his master's servants and did not go down to his house.

10 David was told, 'Uriah did not go home.' So he asked Uriah, 'Haven't you just come from a military campaign? Why didn't you go home?'

11 Uriah said to David, "The ark and Israel and Judah are staying in tents, and my commander Joab and my LORD's men are camped in the open country. How could I go to my house to eat and drink and make love to my wife? As surely as you live, I will not do such a thing!'"

2 SAMUEL 11:5-11

What's happening is David is trying to cover his tracks. He's hoping Uriah would go home and sleep with his wife and then the pregnancy would appear to be his own child. But Uriah refuses to go home and enjoy these luxuries of life while the rest of the army is still on the battlefield. What Uriah is doing is desiring to demonstrate a level of honor, integrity, and character to honor King David, Joab, and his army companions.

What we see is Uriah who demonstrates a level of integrity and character that we wish David had demonstrated. On the other hand, David is revealing his character right now. And his character is coming up short of his level of success. It's so far off kilter that his immediate response to his big mistake is to try to cover it up with another lie.

I've had a few friends over the years who have come to me admitting that their life was crashing in some significant way. They had fallen to a significant sin, their marriage was about to crash and burn, something had been discovered and they were losing their job, or something to that level of significance. In each case I remember the individuals pointing to a few small things that had gotten off balance in their lives. Those small things, when not tended, lead to big things.

Quite frankly, if you bend on the small things now, you'll crash on the big things later.

How do we keep our eyes open for this hidden mine?

DAILY DISCOVERY/ SKEPTIC'S CHALLENGE: Ask yourself, are you bending on any small things now? Ask yourself, if you had significant influence or success, would your character be where you would want it, to be able to handle the weight of it? Where do you think you need to shore up your character? Who will you talk to about the strengths and weaknesses of your character today?

NOTES

WEEK TWELVE / DAY THREE

THE HIDDEN LANDMINES OF IDENTITY: HIDDEN SIN

"Everyone who does evil hates the light, and will not come into the light for fear that their deeds will be exposed."

JOHN 3:20

"But everything exposed by the light becomes visible—and everything that is illuminated becomes a light."

EPHESIANS 5:13

"Therefore confess your sins to each other and pray for each other so that you may be healed. The prayer of a righteous person is powerful and effective."

JAMES 5:16

One day, as a young boy, I was roughhousing my way through our dining room and hit the wall in some way and knocked over several of my mom's Hummels. If you're unaware, Hummels are small, over-priced porcelain figurines. As a small child I'm pretty sure I precariously balanced the broken-off heads back on top of their fractured bodies and hoped no one would notice. I don't know how long it took until my mom noticed and the questions began. "Who broke my Hummels?" Mom asked with a look of fury on her face. Each child denied it. Of course, my two older siblings denied it truthfully and I denied it with a lie. It doesn't take much for a parent to see through the lies of a young child, and while I probably thought I was holding up well, I'm sure I was ridiculously floundering in my lie. My parents didn't let it go, they kept asking more and more questions until I'm sure I found myself flustered, confused, and eventually heartbroken for lying to them. I broke down in tears, confessed what happened, and I'm sure I received a punishment. But that confession also began the healing process.

My parents glued the heads back onto the Hummels, and while they probably lost all their value, for years as I would pass by these figurines, they provided me with the most valuable message a kid could receive. A tangible image of the lesson of concealing a sin, having it discovered, but the discovery process not being as bad as I thought it would be, and the healing process quicker and more life giving than I imagined.

This leads to the fourth hidden landmine of identity:

Landmine #4: Hidden Sin.

We'll pick up the story of David where we left off. David is trying to cover up his sin with Bathsheba by trying to get Uriah to sleep with his wife and this accidental pregnancy will appear to be his own child.

12 "Then David said to him, 'Stay here one more day, and tomorrow I will send you back.' So Uriah remained in Jerusalem that day and the next.
13 At David's invitation, he ate and drank with him, and David made him drunk. But in the evening Uriah went out to sleep on his mat among his master's servants; he did not go home.
14 In the morning David wrote a letter to Joab and sent it with Uriah.
15 In it he wrote, 'Put Uriah out in front where the fighting is fiercest. Then withdraw from him so he will be struck down and die.'
2 SAMUEL 11:12-15

So David tries repeatedly to get Uriah to go home and sleep with his wife Bathsheba and in verse 13, David even gets Uriah drunk to try to pull off his cover-up plan. But to no avail. So in an effort to keep his sin covered, David goes as far as rationalizing murder. Uriah ends up carrying his own execution letter to the commander of the army while he's trying his best to be honorable to his nation, his God, and his king.

What it shows us is what lengths we will go to cover up our sins.

There is a counterintuitive truth about hidden sin. The moment hidden sin is revealed is the moment freedom and healing can begin.

A few years ago one of my friends lost his job, nearly his marriage, and his reputation, all due to a hidden addiction and sin. He later told me the best day of his life was the day the truth came out. This individual wasn't even caught, he was just so worn out from living the lie. The best thing was when it was no longer hidden.

There is nothing that will drain your soul more than trying to maintain a hidden sin.

James 5:16 says, "Therefore confess your sins to each other and pray for each other so that you may be healed..."

When we bring sin into the light, we actually initiate the healing process.

If your soul is weary and worn from concealing a hidden lie or sin, might I encourage you that today can be your day to start your healing. Don't continue to dance around this dangerous mine in your life. Dig it up, drag it out, and disarm it before something blows.

DAILY DISCOVERY/ SKEPTIC'S CHALLENGE: Do you have a hidden sin? Does anyone know? Is anyone helping you toward freedom? If you are at a place where it still seems small, this is when we often think, "It's not worth telling anyone." But the truth is right now, while things are not out of control, is the best time to bring it to the light and deal with it.

If it is out of control, there is still a way for freedom. While it may be a difficult road, I'd encourage you to take a big bold step today and tell someone. Find a local Celebrate Recovery group to help you walk into freedom. If you have a small group, tell at least one person in your group. This may be the scariest and bravest thing you ever do in your life. Do it! Confront and expose what is hidden, and start your healing today.

WEEK TWELVE / DAY FOUR

THE HIDDEN LANDMINES OF IDENTITY: LIES AND TWISTED TRUTHS

"Truthful lips will endure forever,
But a lying tongue is only for a moment."
PROVERBS 12:19 (NASB)

"A truthful witness saves lives,
But one who declares lies is deceitful."
PROVERBS 14:25 (NASB)

"One who practices deceit will not dwell within my house;
One who speaks lies shall not maintain his position before me."
PSALM 101:7 (NASB)

"If we say that we have fellowship with Him and yet walk in the darkness,
we lie and do not practice the truth."
1 JOHN 1:6 (NASB)

Some people are directionally challenged and others are fairly directionally savvy. I consider myself to be of the latter group. So when I got my north, south, east, and west all turned around and backward in my hometown growing up, it really threw me for a loop. I knew where everything was located, but my north compass was upside down. One day I got into a conversation with a family member about where a store was located. I kept saying, "You go north up this road until it runs into another (specific) road." To which they said, "That's not north, that would be heading south." To which I replied, "No, that's north." "No, that's south," they rebutted. Back and forth we went until we pulled out a map—remember those big paper maps? And sure enough, they were right. That was the day I realized the internal map in my head had been wrong for all those years.

My biggest problem was that I believed so strongly that my directions were correct. I believed a lie. And even though I had a conviction of belief, I had a conviction of belief around something that wasn't true.

This is the fifth hidden landmine of identities:

Landmine #5: Belief in a lie or twisted truth.

We're rejoining our story with King David. He's already been trying to cover up his sin with Bathsheba and the pregnancy that resulted. He's tried to get Uriah to sleep with his wife so it would look like his own child. When that doesn't work, David decides to scheme a plan which will result in Uriah's death. Let's join the story in 2 Samuel 11.

16 "So while Joab had the city under siege, he put Uriah at a place where he knew the strongest defenders were. 17 When the men of the city came out and fought against Joab, some of the men in David's army fell; moreover, Uriah the Hittite died.
18 Joab sent David a full account of the battle." 2 SAMUEL 11:16-18

"25 David told the messenger, 'Say this to Joab: 'Don't let this upset you; the sword devours one as well as another. Press the attack against the city and destroy it.' Say this to encourage Joab.'
26 When Uriah's wife heard that her husband was dead, she mourned for him. 27 After the time of mourning was over, David had her brought to his house, and she became his wife and bore him a son. But the thing David had done displeased the LORD." 2 SAMUEL 11:25-27

At this point in the story, I think David is believing his own lie. I think he's believing that he got away with it, or that this all worked out well in the end.

Sure, some people died, but David got the girl and it appears like life will just move on for David and Bathsheba. The problem is when we start believing our own lies, or even twisted truths, it will eventually catch up with us and lead to our downfalls.

Even for me, believing my north was north when it was truly south eventually caught up to me. There was no way my incorrect belief would hold up forever.

David had experienced the favor of God upon him for much of his life. Even though God's favor upon him was true, there was a misapplication to that truth. Maybe David thought that God's favor would be upon him forever, no matter what he did, almost like God's favor couldn't be lost for him. The twisted application was that David was acting like a king: completely unrestricted as if God would bless everything he did. Unfortunately, it wasn't true. God was not going to continue to bless David if he walked in reckless disobedience.

What could be a lie that takes hold of us and robs us of a healthy identity? How about the lie that no one can truly be trusted. Perhaps, up until now in life, everyone has let you down. So you decide it's not safe to open yourself up to others, and instead lead a life of isolation. In the process you cut yourself off from all the promises of God that come from the "one anothers" in scripture. There are over 40 "one anothers" of the blessings to receive when we have others in our lives. It's a simple lie, that when believed, can set your identity on a track to destruction.

Or how about a twisted truth? Consider the statement, "There can be freedom from addiction for them." While that is true, the twist to that truth is to see it for "them" and never for you. Believing that you can never find freedom from an addiction is like a self-fulfilling prophecy. You never will. Twisted truth is believing something that is true, but misapplying it.

I imagine David believed God's favor was with him. That was true. But it was misapplied if he thought he could live however he wanted without repercussions.

Are there any lies or twisted truths in your life that could have you on a path toward a hidden mine?

DAILY DISCOVERY: Are there any truths about God or promises for His people that you think don't apply to you? Do you think you are the exception to the rule? Are there things you believe that you can't find support for in the Bible? Ask God to reveal to you any lies you've been believing or truths you've been misapplying. Write down whatever He brings to mind, then ask Him what the truth is and how it can set you free.

SKEPTIC'S CHALLENGE/ PRAYER: Are there any "always," "only," or "never" statements you've believed over yourself? "I'll always struggle with my addiction." "I'm the only person dealing with this." "I'll never have any trusted friends." These extreme statements that lead to defeat, isolation, or hopelessness are always lies. Are there any statements you've believed that perhaps have you stalled out, or on a trajectory toward a hidden mine? If God could be real and has a dream for some freedom in your life, what might He be saying to you today?

NOTES

WEEK TWELVE / DAY FIVE

THE HIDDEN LANDMINES OF IDENTITY: A NON-TEACHABLE SPIRIT

"My sacrifice, O God, is a broken spirit;
a broken and contrite heart
you, God, will not despise."

PSALM 51:17

I remember a specific day from many years ago as if it were yesterday. It was the day I shared with my wife, my best friend, and my boss some of the landmines I had discovered in my life. There were some landmines that, if not brought to the light and disarmed, could have resulted in the loss of my ministry, my marriage, and my life as I knew it. That was the day freedom and healing began for me.

Now, years later, the landscape of my life is very different, and the landmines are targeted differently, but I'm still looking for them and continually have to dig them up and disarm them before they hurt me or others.

One of the most important character traits to discovering landmines and disarming them is the belief that "you too have places to grow." If you can carry a teachable spirit throughout life, you'll discover there is always something more to learn and always some way to grow.

The opposite mindset is the final hidden landmine to our identities.

Landmine #6: A non-teachable spirit.

This is one huge redeeming character trait of King David. Up until now, David is scheming, conniving, lying and plotting, but that will all come to an end with the confrontation of the prophet Nathan.

In 2 Samuel 12, the prophet Nathan goes nose to nose with David. He tells a really creative story to help David see how wrong his behaviors have been. You should read it for yourself in 2 Samuel 12:1-9. But here's the most important part. How will David respond? Will he deny Nathan's confrontation? Will he have Nathan killed? (Because as the king he could have done that and no one would have questioned him.) No, instead look at how David responds:

"Then David said to Nathan, 'I have sinned against the LORD.'"

2 SAMUEL 12:13

One of David's most redeeming character traits is that he demonstrates a broken and contrite heart and a teachable spirit.

As Psalm 51:17 says, "a broken and contrite heart you, God, will not despise."

One of the greatest things about God is that He will always give you another chance if you come to Him with a broken heart and teachable spirit.

On the flip side, if you're not teachable you are setting yourself up for destruction. You might as well just start preparing for something to blow up in your life.

But please, might I challenge you, stay teachable. Look for places to grow, change and mature. Be quick to admit that there are places to improve. Be ready to apologize and own your mistakes, flaws, and shortcomings. These are the traits that will help you discover the hidden landmines in your life and walk you into a healthy and God-given identity.

DAILY DISCOVERY/ SKEPTIC'S CHALLENGE: If you know of a landmine from this week that you haven't yet addressed, be teachable around it and tell someone about it. Then form a plan and get help as necessary to deal with the landmines in your life. Help and healing is on the other side of dealing with the landmines in our lives. You can wait to stumble across them or you can deal with them directly. Dig them up, deal with them! You'll be glad you did!

WEEK TWELVE / DAY SIX & SEVEN

DAY 6: LET THAT THOUGHT SIMMER

What idea was most challenging to you this week?

DAY 7: LET THAT THOUGHT SIMMER

What day from this week or concept do you want to rethink about?

WHERE FROM HERE?

You made it to the end of our 12-week experiment and journey.
Way to go!

Have you ever made it to the end of a significant commitment and asked,
"What now?"

Earlier this year our staff had our own weight loss competition. It was
perfectly placed. We started early in the year, and ended at a time that
set all of us up for feeling healthier and looking better as we headed into
spring and summer. When we set our sights on a goal, both Lisa and
I can be pretty competitive and serious about hitting it. So with this
competition we were not messing around. It was a ten-week competition.
And for ten weeks we worked all the dieting angles such as eliminating
all sugar, nuts, and dairy and intermittent fasting. To say the least, for
those 10 weeks, Lisa and I were fat-burning machines. But then you'll
never guess what happened. The competition ended and I came in
second to another staff member. I'm not bitter...

But the diet was over.

Now if you've ever dieted to a deadline, let me just warn you there is a
major danger in that approach. Why? Because we did what most people
would do who diet to a deadline. We celebrated our weight loss and
great accomplishments by going out to eat. And boy did we eat. That's
right, we ate the dinner rolls, we ate the appetizer, we ate the entree, we
ate the dessert, we had the post-meal cup of coffee, and we even stopped
at a gas station on the way home just to buy some of our favorite candy.
And as we lounged around the house that night, we topped it all off with
some popcorn. We ended that diet and ended it with a bang. My biggest
problem was the day after. Why? Because the day after, I didn't have a
plan. And since I didn't have a plan, I went back to my pre-competition

eating habits. Which weren't horrible, but also weren't the best.

All that to say, my hope and prayer is that you've created some great habits in your life, meeting with God, searching for Him, and discovering different aspects of who He is and who He says you are. The worst thing you can do at this point is say, "That was nice, now back to the way things were." Instead of digressing to old thought patterns or habits, might I challenge you to press in and continue your journey with Him.

So, how do I do that? Where do I go from here?

From here, you'll want to get into a strategic plan that will continue to push your faith, grow your knowledge of God, and continue to stretch you. This past year, this is something that our staff at Lakeland has taken very seriously.

We've created a self-guided, digital-platform discipleship pathway. Simply put, it's a strategic plan for helping you take your next spiritual step on your spiritual journey. And it's designed for everyone, no matter where you are.

It's for the skeptic, seeker, and non-believer. It's for the spiritual infant (or newbie). It's for the spiritual child (the one who is learning quickly and starting to grow). It is for the spiritual young adult and spiritual parent. And for each stage in the spiritual journey we've created video content and field guides with over 12 months of strategic steps and learning for you right where you're at.

If you're a skeptic and you've wondered, if there is absolute truth, can the Bible be trusted, what is the true essence of church and why does it matter; all these types of questions and more are answered and set up for you to further explore.

If you're new to the faith, this pathway will lead you to strategically tackle subjects around baptism, how to read and study the Bible, how to pray, why community matters and how to best grow, etc.

And if you continue on the pathway it will take you all the way to discovering your spiritual gifts, equipping you to talk about faith with others, serving in and outside the church, hearing the voice of God, and so much more.

Just like we don't want to diet to a deadline and then go back to old patterns in our lives, I hope God has touched your life in such a profound way that you don't want to go back to old patterns. So don't. Instead, take another step in your journey. Continue the experiment by continuing to grow. Take your next step on the pathway.

To discover more about the discipleship pathway and take your next step, go to www.lakeland.church.